Vic Hadfield's Diary
From Moscow to the Play-offs

Vic Hadfield's Diary

FROM MOSCOW
TO THE PLAY-OFFS

By Vic Hadfield
With Tim Moriarty

Doubleday & Company, Inc.
Garden City, New York
1974

ISBN: 0-385-06849-2
Library of Congress Catalog Card Number 73-83637
Copyright © 1974 by Tim Moriarty and Vic Hadfield Enterprises Ltd.
All Rights Reserved
Printed in the United States of America
Published simultaneously in hardcover and paperback
First Edition

To my family, friends, and fans . . .
All those who stood behind me

Editor's Foreword

Vic Hadfield is no newcomer to pro hockey. He has been playing in the National Hockey League since 1961, when he joined the New York Rangers as a rough-hewn youngster with close-cropped blond hair and a short temper. His hair is longer now and so is the fuse attached to his temper. He'll still fight at the drop of a hockey stick, but only if provoked.

As a reporter covering Ranger games for the past twenty-five years, I have watched the transformation of Vic Hadfield from a red-necked rookie to a seasoned, fifty-goal-scoring pro. He has always impressed me with his forthrightness, his quick wit, and his native intelligence.

When I approached Vic in the summer of '72 and suggested he keep a diary of the Rangers' 1972–73 season, he accepted my proposal with genuine enthusiasm. Neither of us realized at the time what a strange season Vic was about to experience.

It started with Team Canada's historic series against the Russians in September. Vic became the storm center of a swirling controversy when he left the team in Moscow and returned home, embittered by a clash with coach Harry Sinden.

In *Hockey Showdown*, an earlier book published by Doubleday, Sinden related his version of the incident.

Hadfield's rebuttal is included in the early part of this book. It makes interesting reading and provides food for thought for those fans who were quick to admonish Hadfield and label him a quitter.

As the season progressed, I felt compassion for the Rangers' team captain. Memories of the flight from Moscow no longer haunted him; the torture he now was experiencing was physical, not mental. He suffered through a series of injuries: an aching shoulder, two busted fingers, a sore knee, a deep stick cut above his left eye, and a severe concussion.

It was the concussion that caused him the most misery. It affected his vision and his equilibrium; it produced persistent headaches and nausea. Vic played many games over the final five weeks of the regular season on sheer guts; he should have been resting in a hospital, but he felt the team needed him, so he insisted on playing.

Throughout all this travail, Vic Hadfield never lost his sense of humor. I remember a day in early March when, concerned over the aftereffects of the concussion, he visited a neurologist, who examined Vic for possible brain damage. "The doc told me there's nothing loose upstairs," he said. "I still have all my marbles."

Vic Hadfield chuckled. That's one of his greatest assets —the ability to laugh in the face of pain and agony.

It is hoped the reader will get an occasional chuckle out of Vic Hadfield's diary, and also come to recognize the undeniable courage of the Rangers' "Captain Courageous."

TIM MORIARTY
Rockville Centre, N.Y.

The Russians are coming, the Russians are coming.

You better believe it. After months of negotiations, the bloody Russians have finally agreed to match their best hockey team—a bunch of pros masquerading as amateurs —against a group of National Hockey League All-Stars.

It's all settled. There will be four games in Canada beginning in early September, then four games in Moscow in late September. I accepted an invitation last month to play for Team Canada—the official name of our squad.

The temperature was in the low eighties when I checked into the Sutton Hotel in Toronto today with other members of Team Canada. Nice weather for swimming or fishing or boating on Lake Ontario. But the hell with that. It's time to play hockey.

We take our physical exams tomorrow at Maple Leaf Gardens. Then the big push starts. We've got less than three weeks to prepare for the series opener in Montreal September 2.

All the big guns of the NHL are here. Phil Esposito and Wayne Cashman of the Bruins, Yvan Cournoyer and Frank Mahovlich of the Canadiens, Ron Ellis and Paul Henderson of the Maple Leafs, Dennis Hull and Stan Mikita of the Black Hawks, and my two linemates on the Rangers, Jean Ratelle and Rod Gilbert.

But pro hockey's most famous Bobbys—Orr and Hull—

are missing. Orr had knee surgery in June and isn't ready to skate yet. Hull isn't eligible for Team Canada because he jumped to the World Hockey Association in June for tons of money and half the wheat in the province of Manitoba.

I was chatting with Ratelle and Gilbert earlier today and they agreed with me that the WHA players shouldn't have been blackballed. We thought this was going to be a Canada vs. Russia series. So why not let Bobby Hull and Gerry Cheevers and a couple of those other WHA jumpers play? They didn't surrender their Canadian citizenship when they joined the new league, did they?

AUGUST 21

We've been practicing now for a week at Maple Leaf Gardens. The first days at camp were just like any other hockey camp. We did a lot of free skating and limbering up because most of us hadn't been on skates for three months. All the fellows are working hard. We know the Russians will be totally prepared or they wouldn't have agreed to play us.

Gilbert, Ratelle, and I have been playing together on a line. We have already played some intrasquad games and were told our line was probably the best in camp. Harry Sinden, who came out of retirement to coach Team Canada, has told us he plans to use our line as a unit against the Russians.

I don't know Sinden too well. When he was coaching the Bruins I heard stories about him—some good, some bad. But I don't believe I ever talked to him until this summer when he called me at my home in Oakville and invited me to join Team Canada. I said I'd be happy to represent my country, but I told him I needed a couple of days before giving him an answer because I had a few things to straighten out.

I wanted to be sure first that all the top players in the NHL would be invited. Also, I have an investment at home in which I have sunk a lot of money. Andy Bathgate and I are building an eighteen-hole golf course at Burlington, Ontario, not far from my home. We had to put up a half million dollars for this venture. So before making a final commitment to play for Team Canada I had to make sure that Andy could carry on for me while I was away.

Andy and I are old friends going back to the days when he played for the Rangers. He said he would be able to handle things while I was away. I then talked it over with my wife, Myrna. I would be giving up several weeks of the summer, and this is the time when I like to enjoy life with Myrna and our son and two daughters. Myrna knew how much I wanted to play for Team Canada and didn't offer any objections.

Word then got out that I was taking two or three days to make a decision. The local newspaper in Oakville printed a story that claimed I wasn't interested in playing for Team Canada. This was a lie.

About a week later I received another phone call from Sinden.

"What's your decision, Vic?" he asked.

"I'm ready to play those Russians tomorrow," I said.

"Good," Sinden said. "I'll mail you all the instructions we have prepared for the players in a couple of days. Stay in shape."

He laughed and added, "I'm not worried about you. I know you'll stay in shape working on that golf course."

Harry Sinden sounded friendly over the phone and seemed pleased to have me on Team Canada.

SEPTEMBER 1

Hey, the Canadians are coming. Hell, we're already here.

We flew from Toronto to Montreal earlier today on

3

two chartered flights. We play our opening game against the Russians tomorrow night at the Montreal Forum. That place will really be jumping.

We're staying at the Château Champlain, a great hotel. My roomie is Brad Park, that kid with the large ears. His wife, Gerry, is expecting their first child any day now. Expecting? Jeez, she's about two weeks overdue, and Brad is acting like a cat on a hot tin roof.

"Take it easy," I told him while we were having dinner tonight. "I've been through this three times. There's nothing to it."

"Sure, sure," Brad said. "You veterans are all the same. But I'll bet you were just as nervous before your first kid was born."

He's right. I was worried when Myrna was giving birth to Michele, our first child, in 1961. I was just as nervous when Julie was born in 1962 and when Jeffrey was born in 1964. You're never a veteran in that league.

So while Gerry Park is back in Toronto, sweating it out, her husband is here, sweating it out. And Brad and I both have to worry about that opening game against the Russians.

The excitement is really building now. Newspapermen from all over North America—and some from Europe—have arrived for this Canadian-Russian confrontation. It's a first—sort of hockey "cold war."

At practice this afternoon at the Forum, our opening lineups were printed on a bulletin board in the dressing room. I'll be playing on a line with Rod and Jean. Good deal. We know each other's moves so well after playing together on the Rangers for six years . . . this has to help us.

But what will the Russians really be like? How will they play us? We've heard all those rumors about them; how they can't skate or shoot with pros like us. We had men scouting them in Russia and they came back telling us that if we don't win every game by five or six goals there is something wrong with our hockey club—or maybe our way of life.

Sinden claims the Russian goaltenders are weak. In a newspaper release the other day, Sinden said, "The Russian goalies don't seem to have improved nearly as much as the rest of their players since I played against them in 1958 and 1960. The goalies look weak trying to glove rising shots from twenty-five to thirty feet. The Russians also have a flagrant defect in the way they kill penalties. That's something our guys will be able to work on easily."

SEPTEMBER 3

Those damn Russians played hockey last night like they invented it instead of us. They waxed us pretty good. We got beat, 7–3.

One reporter called it "another Dunkirk." A New York writer likened it to Pearl Harbor. It was a little bit of both. It was a national catastrophe.

The Russians played well and showed a lot of bounce. Phil Esposito put us ahead with a goal after only thirty seconds. Paul Henderson scored six minutes later. Now we're leading, 2–0, but the Russians don't panic. They tie the score before the end of the first period, then Valeri Kharlamov scores two goals in the second period. That would have been enough to insure the Russians the victory, but they beat Ken Dryden three more times in a five-minute span in the final period.

When we flew back to Toronto today to prepare for the second game at Maple Leaf Gardens tomorrow night you'd think we had just lost the Third World War. Everybody was asking, "What happened?" They couldn't believe that the Russians had beaten us.

5

The Canadian public had been misled by what had been printed in the newspapers. Maybe we, the players, had been misled, too. Everybody expected us to win that first game by five or six goals. When we lost, it was total havoc.

And the newspaper criticism was brutal. The fans and the writers who we thought were going to be behind us . . . well, they just turned their backs on us. We learned then that we would be on our own, that we weren't going to receive any support from most of our own people.

We practiced after arriving back in Toronto this afternoon. After practice, Jean, Rod, and I found out we wouldn't be playing in the second game. Our line didn't play particularly well in the first game, but neither did the other lines. We realize others are waiting to play, but I didn't expect our whole line to be benched. What the hell, this makes us look like scapegoats.

The news wasn't all bad, though. Gerry Park presented Brad with a son late this afternoon. They're going to name the little guy James Edmund Park. Gerry came through the ordeal okay. So did Brad. So light up the cigars for little Jamie. He's got great parents.

SEPTEMBER 5

Who said the Russians were unbeatable? We won the second game last night, 4–1. And guess who set up the first two goals by Phil Esposito and Yvan Cournoyer? That new poppa, Brad Park. The Mahovlich brothers got the other two goals and Tony Esposito handled the goaltending. Tony was super.

There was no booing in Toronto. Maybe it's because we never trailed in the game. The fans had to cheer; they had no reason to boo.

We're now in Winnipeg, where we play the third game tomorrow night. On the flight out here we ran into Bobby

Hull. His wife was with him. They were telling us about moving into a new house in Winnipeg, where Bobby will be the player-coach of the WHA team. Bobby wished us luck in the series. What a man.

At practice today I checked the bulletin board in the dressing room. My name wasn't in the lineup again. Neither was Rod's. What the hell is going on here?

Those who won't be playing tomorrow night stayed on the ice longer to practice. There were ten or twelve of us, including Rod, Rich Martin, Gil Perreault, Don Awrey, Dennis Hull, and Eddie Johnston. We call ourselves the "Black Aces," which is a name used to describe the subs or part-timers on hockey teams.

On the bus ride back to the North Star Inn in Winnipeg, the "Black Aces" did a lot of joking around. Somebody—I can't remember who it was—wisecracked, "Hey, Vic, the next game you play will be in Sweden." I laughed but I must admit it was a nervous laugh.

SEPTEMBER 7

We tied the Russians, 4–4, last night and now the spit has really hit the fan. Maybe we should have won after getting a 4–2 lead in the second period, but the criticism I've heard and read is unbelievable. You'd think we were in a foreign country.

One guy wrote that we weren't interested in beating the Russians—that all we were interested in was booze and broads. Now, how would you like to have children back home reading that guff about their fathers? It made us all sick because it was so untrue. We wanted to beat the Russians so much we could taste it.

After checking into Vancouver today we held a team meeting. We wanted to get a few things cleared up before the fourth game here tomorrow night. It hurt a lot of the fellows to think they had given up all this time—a good chunk of their summer vacation—and now found the fans and the writers weren't behind them. What a rude awakening we got. So we talked it over and realized we were in this mess together and would have to pull together.

SEPTEMBER 9

Another debacle. The Russians beat us for the second time, 5–3. This time they got an early jump on Ken Dryden, beating him twice in the first seven minutes. We had to play catch-up hockey the rest of the night and couldn't close the gap.

Rod and I played but Ratelle didn't. I couldn't understand Sinden not using Ratty. He had played a helluva game in Winnipeg. He scored a goal and looked like the old Ratty.

The Vancouver fans booed us almost from the moment we skated onto the ice. I glanced at some of our guys on the bench and they all had puzzled looks on their faces. They couldn't believe what was happening.

Phil Esposito went on television after the game and blasted the fans for their lack of support. Phil has been working his butt off in this series, but the fans have been riding him, too. When he got back to the dressing room, Phil received some phone calls from friends. One was from a lady who called all the way from Nova Scotia. She told Phil to tell us not to give up, that she was with us all the way.

Well, it's nice to know there are a few people in Canada who don't think we're bums.

SEPTEMBER 12

We've had a few days off to rest up for the second half of the series. We leave later this week for Sweden. We'll

8

spend almost a week there, play a couple of exhibition games and then move on to Moscow. The series resumes there on September 22.

It hasn't been too pleasant around the Toronto area since we returned from Vancouver. Everybody is yapping about how we should have won all four games in Canada handily instead of settling for a victory and a tie. We're just as disappointed as the fans, but not discouraged. We can still turn it around during those four games in Moscow.

I didn't like sitting out two of the first four games. I come to play and when I have to sit, I fret.

One newspaper recently quoted Sinden as saying I had a bad attitude. What the hell does he mean by that? If wanting to play represents a bad attitude, then I'm really in trouble.

SEPTEMBER 18

We have been in Stockholm for almost a week and leave tomorrow for Moscow. The idea behind our stopover here was to get in a couple of warmups against the Swedish national team and to become accustomed to the larger ice surface on these European rinks. But scheduling exhibitions against the Swedes was a big mistake. We all got a chance to play, but we're lucky some of us weren't maimed for life.

The Swedes do a lot of spearing and kicking. In the first game, which we won, 4–1, one of the Swedish defensemen skated up to me and speared me in the stomach. It wasn't an accident. He was trying to injure me. I retaliated by whacking him across the ankle with my stick. Down he went. I thought I had cut off one of his ankles. He was holding it and rolling around on the ice. I got two minutes for slashing; he wasn't even penalized. And the SOB didn't miss a shift for the rest of the game, so he obviously had been faking injury.

9

The second game here was just as rough. I wasn't even near the puck when a Swedish player comes up and with an axlike motion slashes me across the arm. I retaliated this time by clipping him in the nose. He was quite an actor. He skated around the ice pointing to his bloody nose. Then he stood in front of the TV cameras and did the same thing.

In the newspapers the next day I was referred to as an animal. They said I should be barred from hockey. They said the same things about Wayne Cashman. He got into a fight with Ulf Sterner, who once played for the Rangers. Sterner stuck the blade of his stick into Cashman's mouth and left Cash with a sliced tongue. Nice guys.

Being referred to as savages in the Swedish press was bad enough, but it really hurt when some Canadian papers printed those charges. The real truth was never published. The newspapers never mentioned what started these brawls. Ron Ellis was jumped from behind and kicked in the head. That was never mentioned. But on the taped replays on TV you could see the Swedes spearing and kicking.

This is where a lot of the trouble started. Some of our own players started to criticize others on the team for reacting to all the rough stuff. What else could we do? I've always played aggressive hockey, but I never had to resort to the retaliatory methods I used in those Stockholm games.

Even our own team doctor got into the act. He is Dr. Jim Murray of Toronto, and he was quoted as saying he was ashamed to be a Canadian and to be associated with Team Canada. He scolded Dale Tallon, who was cross-checked from behind, then went after the Swede who did it. Tallon turned on Dr. Murray in the dressing room and said, "Get the hell out of here before I punch you in the nose."

Dr. Murray complained about Tallon to Alan Eagleson, who is acting as major domo for Team Canada.

All of this criticism and dissension keeps mounting and we haven't even reached Moscow. You can see it all coming to a head.

SEPTEMBER 20

Welcome to Moscow. Uuggh. It's all a little drab, including our hotel. We're staying at the Intourist. Our wives were waiting for us when we checked in.

Our accommodations at the Intourist leave a lot to be desired. The rooms are small, the beds look like cots, and some are placed so husband and wife sleep toe-to-toe. Now, isn't that a helluva note.

There must be a lot of thieves in Moscow. We brought our own beef with us—a lot of steaks—and they've been stolen. So has the Canadian beer, which we had shipped here. Everybody suspects sabotage. Paul Henderson of the Maple Leafs is convinced our rooms are bugged. "If they are, the Russian commissars aren't going to like some of the things they hear," Richard Martin of the Sabres said.

Martin is a comical kid. While we were in Stockholm, he went around talking with a Swedish accent. When we got on the team bus here, he got down on his hands and knees to inspect the bottom of the bus.

"What the hell are you doing down there, Rich?" I asked.

"I'm checking for a bomb," he said.

That really broke up the guys. We had a bomb scare at our hotel in Stockholm, and most of us don't trust the Russians any more than the Swedes.

SEPTEMBER 22

I've had it with Team Canada. I've got my bags packed and I'm headed home. I'm tired of the deceit, the lies, and the broken promises.

I made this decision after our first practice at the Sports Palace yesterday morning. We were skating around, just limbering up and getting used to the rink when Harry Sinden called us to center ice.

"We'll start out with some line rushes," he said.

Sinden called off eight forward lines—a total of twenty-four players—and didn't call my name. Then he turned to me and said, "Vic, you stand by the boards while the rest practice." I was mystified and a little embarrassed. I could see from the looks on the faces of the other guys that they were dumfounded, too, at what was happening.

After standing there for about thirty minutes, Sinden skated over to me. He wanted me to take a couple of shifts at center.

"What the hell is going on, Harry?" I said. "I'm not a center. I'm a left wing and should be practicing with them."

Sinden shouted, "If you don't like it, Vic, you can take off your equipment."

Now I was really hot. First Sinden had snubbed me as a player and now he was telling me I wasn't good enough to practice with the team at my own position. I didn't take off my equipment, though, as Sinden ordered. I waited until the team had finished practicing, then skated for about twenty-five minutes by myself.

Eagleson was at the rink, so I approached him and asked him what was going on.

"I'm ready to play, but it looks like I'm not needed," I said.

Eagleson tried to pass the buck. "I don't like to interfere," he said. "But I'll talk it over with Harry and meet you back at the hotel."

When I got back to the hotel, Myrna was standing near the elevator. She had just returned from a bus tour of Moscow.

"We're going home," I said.

Myrna had a puzzled look on her face.

"You mean the whole team?" she asked.

"No, just you and me."

We went upstairs and I told her about the incident at practice. Later in the day I had another talk with Eagleson.

I said, "Al, I've got to have some assurance that I'm going to play in Moscow. If Sinden ignores me like that in practice, he obviously isn't planning on using me. Why bring me all the way to Russia just to make a fool of me? I've got the Rangers and the new season to think about. I want to be in shape when the season starts, and I'm not getting in shape here."

Eagleson hemmed and hawed some more. He said, "I don't know why Harry isn't using you. At the beginning of this trip we decided that even if we were losing 19–0 everybody would get a chance to play at least one game in Moscow."

"But I can't even practice with the team," I said.

"Sit tight," Eagleson said. "I'll straighten this out with Harry."

After a couple of more hours of waiting around it became obvious that Eagleson and Sinden were giving me a fast shuffle. All I wanted from them was an indication on whether or not I was going to play in Moscow. When I didn't get it, I asked Eagleson to book me on the next flight home.

There were no flights available yesterday, so we had to spend another night in Moscow. Before leaving this morning, I met some of the players. Some thought I was injured and that was the reason I was heading home. When they learned I wasn't injured, they couldn't figure out why Sinden ignored me in practice. They said they would have done the same thing if Sinden treated them that way.

That's when I learned I wasn't the only unhappy player

13

on Team Canada. Ten others said they were ready to quit for various reasons. When I got down to the hotel lobby this morning, Richard Martin and Josh Guèvremont were there. They had their bags packed and were joining me on the trip home. There would have been more, but the other dissatisfied players—fellows like Don Awrey, Eddie Johnston, and Dennis Hull—feared being criticized.

So it's goodbye Moscow and Team Canada and Harry Sinden. I'm heading home knowing I'm going to face a little flak, but a man must have the courage of his convictions. I feel I made the right decision.

SEPTEMBER 24

I've been home two days and the flak has been heavier than I imagined. The criticism in the Toronto papers has been real cruel. There is no basis of fact for some of the stories being written.

What annoys me is that I was double-crossed by Eagleson, too. When the Canadian writers learned I was leaving Team Canada, they came to me before I went to the airport and asked why. I was about to explain the situation to them when Eagleson interrupted us and said he would take the reporters aside after I left and iron out things so there would be very little static.

I trusted Eagleson and he let me down. I found out later he never talked to the reporters. He never advised them of the real reason I left Team Canada—that I hadn't even been allowed to practice with the team and was given no assurance I would play in Moscow.

So the reporters took it upon themselves to criticize me without learning the facts. They called me a quitter. That was hard to take. I've been playing with the Rangers since 1961, and I'm sure if I was a quitter Emile Francis would never have me on his hockey club or let me serve as cap-

14

tain of the team. Emile knows how to handle men. I can't say the same for Harry Sinden.

Sinden never appeared to know what he was doing as coach of Team Canada. There was too much confusion. He kept screwing around with the lines and had a lot of fellows shaking their heads in dismay. And he played favorites. If you were a friend of Harry's, you played. If you weren't a friend of Harry's, you rode the bench. Gil Perreault quit the day after I left Moscow. He was fed up, too, but I received most of the criticism because I was older and was supposed to be more responsible. Responsible to whom? Certainly not Harry Sinden. I had the guts to turn my back on Sinden; some of the others didn't, though they were just as disgusted with the whole Team Canada setup.

I've been trying to explain my side of the story since I got back, but people won't listen. Even the newspaper here in my hometown of Oakville has raked me over the coals without even checking out the facts. I've lived here all my life, my parents live here, and I like Oakville. But the people never took this into consideration. They've been very cruel.

I can accept criticism, but not the way they handed it out this time. Some of the children in Oakville are as bad as their parents. They have picked on my own children at school, criticizing them for my decision. Small people, small minds.

OCTOBER 1

I'm back with the Rangers and played my first exhibition game with them last night. I scored a goal in our 5–4 victory over the St. Louis Blues. It feels good to be back on a team where there is no bickering, no back-biting.

The series is over in Moscow. Team Canada won the

last three games to pull out the series with four victories, three losses, and a tie. I'm happy for the guys and especially for Paul Henderson, who scored the winning goals in the final three games. I guess you could say Team Canada won in spite of Harry Sinden.

There was a big celebration in Toronto when Team Canada returned home. People who were booing them across Canada at the start were finally cheering the players and jumping back on the bandwagon. I wonder how they would have acted if Team Canada had lost?

It's too bad it had to end this way. So many of the players thought it would be different. The entire organization of Team Canada was handled badly. I know from talking to the players that they will never participate in another series like this unless it is organized differently.

I have received more good mail than bad in the past week. Oh, there have been a few hate letters, but many other people apparently stopped to think and consider the decision I made. They congratulated me for standing by it. They've done a lot to cheer me up in recent days.

OCTOBER 2

We tied the Red Wings, 2–2, in another exhibition last night at Detroit. During the pregame warmups I chatted with Arnie Brown of the Wings.

"Hey, Vic, have you heard anything back in New York about the possibility of my being traded?" Arnie asked.

"Yeah," I said, "the rumor is you're supposed to come back with us."

Arnie smiled. He'd like nothing better than to play for the Rangers again. I'd like it, too. Arnie and I are old friends. We used to ride together to practice before he was traded to Detroit in 1970. We were very close and our wives got along great.

Kenny Hodge cornered me last night at Boston, where we tied the Bruins, 3–3, in our final preseason game. Kenny spent a lot of time in the doghouse when Sinden was coach of the Bruins.

"How do you like Sinden now?" he asked.

I grinned and said, "Now I know why you didn't make Team Canada. Harry picked only his friends."

"You mean you're a friend of Harry's?"

I grinned again. "No longer, Kenny, no longer."

OCTOBER 6

The sparring is over; we open the regular season tomorrow night against the Red Wings at the Olympia. We checked into Detroit in the late afternoon, and now Brad Park and I are stretched out in our beds in the Hotel Pontchartrain watching TV. It's a plush hotel, quite a change from the old Sheraton-Cadillac where we used to stay during our visits to Detroit.

When I first joined the Rangers, our homes away from home weren't too comfortable—mostly second-class hotels with rooms a little bigger than closets. Emile (Cat) Francis has changed all that. We always travel first class now. When we visit Boston, we stay at the Sonesta over in Cambridge. In Oakland it's the Edgewater-Hyatt House. In St. Louis it's the Chase-Park Plaza. We moved out of the Chase once because an ill-advised desk clerk cut off all phone calls to the Cat's room. What a mistake that was. The Cat spends most of his waking hours on the phone.

Two of our regulars, Ted Irvine and Jim Neilson, are on the injured list. Irvine has sprained ligaments in his left knee and Neilson has a broken bone in his right foot.

Brad and I have been looking ahead to the season opener. We know the Red Wings will be a hustling hockey club because they have a hustling coach in Johnny Wilson. Some of his enthusiasm has to rub off on the players.

Most of the experts have picked us to finish first. All the guys realize this, and know we're going to have to get off to a flying start—here in Detroit and Sunday night in Chicago.

Harry Sinden is back with the Bruins. They deserve each other. Sinden did a lot of mouthing off when he quit the Bruins as coach in 1970. He claimed the whole organization was too tight-fisted and cheap. But when the home building outfit Harry had been working for went bankrupt last summer, he decided the Bruins weren't so bad after all. He's been named "managing director" of the Bruins, whatever that means. What it probably means is that he'll be looking over Tom Johnson's shoulder from now on, waiting to reclaim his job as the Bruins' coach. Don't turn your back, Tom.

OCTOBER 8

We stumbled coming out of the gate. The Red Wings put four shots behind Eddie Giacomin in the first period and beat us, 5–3. Steve Vickers got one of our goals in his first NHL game, quite a thrill for him. But the rest of the guys were upset over the loss.

We didn't play well at all, but you have to give credit to the Red Wings. They came out skating and checking. Denis DeJordy looked good in goal. Detroit picked him up from the Islanders in a trade for Arnie Brown. Arnie wasn't happy about the trade. He was hoping if he was traded it would be back to the Rangers. He's back on Long Island, but with the expansion club. That's hockey, Arnie.

Gilles Villemure has an aching wrist, so Giacomin will

be back in goal against the Black Hawks tonight at Chicago Stadium. The Black Hawks will be gunning for us. We beat them four straight in last spring's play-offs, and they've never forgotten that. They have something to prove. They lost Bobby Hull to the WHA, and the experts keep reminding them that without Bobby they're nothing. We'll see.

OCTOBER 9

Oh, my aching back. The Black Hawks beat us, 5–1. We controlled the play in the first period, which ended in a 1–1 tie. Rod Gilbert got our goal. But the Hawks broke it open in the second period. Cliff Koroll beat Giacomin twice in about three minutes. Koroll has always been a good two-way hockey player. He's a lot like Toronto's Ron Ellis—a hard worker. He moves up and down his wing and never strays. Playing with Stan Mikita brings out the best in Koroll. He and Stan play well together. Cliff likes to bust down his wing, skate like hell, and then look for somebody to put the puck on his stick. Stan does that with perfection.

Giacomin isn't happy about giving up ten goals in our first two games. Eddie never complains, though. He could have faulted some of our guys for most of those goals, but he refused to put the blast on anybody. You could see he was seething inside, though. So was our boss.

When we got back to New York around 3:00 A.M., Emile called a surprise practice. He told us to be at Skateland, our practice rink in New Hyde Park, by ten-thirty. As I was coming out of the dressing room and heading for the ice, Frank Paice, our trainer, was coming in. He was carrying a pail of pucks.

"What's up, Frank?" I asked.

"The Cat said no pucks today," Paice answered.

Oh, oh. I knew what that meant. We were going to do nothing but skate, skate, skate.

The Cat pulled a similar drill on us back in 1970. We had lost a Thursday night game at St. Louis. Before returning home the following day, the Cat took us back to St. Louis Arena and had us skate for ninety minutes. We went through every skating drill in the book and some others that the Cat devised on the spot. In our next game, back in New York, we clobbered the Bruins, 8–1.

So as I skated out on the ice at Skateland I remembered St. Louis and mumbled, "Here we go again." This time we skated up and down and around the rink for eighty minutes—not quite as long as that day at St. Louis but just as punishing. Bill Fairbairn started counting our trips around the ice and stopped when he got to fifty-four.

It was some exercise in free skating. Not even the goaltenders were exempt. Giacomin is one of the best-skating goalies in the league, but when I looked at him near the end of the drill his face had turned white.

"How do you feel, Eddie?" I asked.

"I think I'm going to pass out," he said.

That's the way most of us felt, but we wouldn't admit it to the boss. If we had complained, he would have driven us even harder.

There was a lot of grumbling when it was over and we dragged ourselves back to the dressing room. Our home opener is two days away—Wednesday night against Vancouver. Every man on the club is ready to go like hell against the Canucks. We don't want to go through another drill like that.

OCTOBER 12

That skating drill was just what the doctor ordered. Or maybe I should say it was just what the Cat ordered. We

20

beat the Canucks, 5–3. Ah, the sweet smell of success. Rod Gilbert got two goals and Ratty got one. I'm the only member of the line who hasn't scored a goal, but I'm not concerned—yet.

Dunc Wilson was the Canucks' goaltender. I think we've discovered something about him. He seems to have a weakness on shots aimed low on his glove side. Four of the five goals we scored against him went in on that side.

Bruce MacGregor joined Neilson and Irvine on the injury list. Murdoch—that's our nickname for MacGregor—was blind-sided by Jim Hargreaves in the first period and wound up with ligament damage in his right knee. When we returned to the dressing room at the end of the game, Murdoch was sitting with an ice pack on his knee. He said, "As soon as that guy hit me I knew it was bad." How bad is it? "It hurts like hell," Murdoch said.

OCTOBER 14

Our toughest weekend of the new season. We play the Canadiens here in Montreal tonight, then face the Minnesota North Stars at Madison Square Garden tomorrow night. We know the Canadiens will be tough. We eliminated them in the play-offs last spring. They'll have this in the back of their minds and will come out skating.

I'm concerned for another reason. This is my first trip back to play in Canada since I left Team Canada. What type of reaction will I receive? We didn't arrive in Montreal until late last night, so I didn't have a chance to go out and have a few beers with the fellows. I stayed in my room at the Château Champlain and watched a little TV.

When I got up this morning, I went down to the lobby and picked up a Montreal newspaper. There was a story about me and how I had been a thorn in the side of the Canadiens because I had scored some goals against them last season and in the play-offs. They're starting to warm up the natives for my return. The same newspaper also quoted Scotty Bowman, the Montreal coach. He said he had a little surprise for Vic Hadfield. Now, what the hell does he mean by that? I don't know what to expect, but I'd better be prepared for anything.

We had our pregame team meeting at the Forum around noon. I didn't see any reporters around. Too bad. I thought they might give me a hint on what's cooking. But it won't be long now. I'll find out what's up when I return to the Forum for the game.

OCTOBER 15

I got a tremendous reception at the Montreal Forum—all boos. It didn't upset me too much because I've always felt those Montreal fans are like a bunch of sheep. One guy starts booing, then the rest join in. Every time I touched the puck I could hear the catcalls. The fans were hoping I would make a mistake or somebody on the Canadiens would rack me up. The hell with them.

I was more disturbed about losing the game. We played well for half of the first period. I set up a goal by Gilbert that tied the score at 1–1. Marc Tardif scored for Montreal about a minute later. We then made a couple of mental mistakes and the Canadiens beat us badly, 6–1.

Bowman's surprise wasn't much. In matching up the lines, he put Yvan Cournoyer against me. Big deal. Yvan's a great little speedster, but it didn't bother me to be matched against him. I didn't score a goal, but neither did Yvan.

After the game, some of the guys on the team suggested we refuse to talk to the Montreal reporters. I told them that would be wrong, that I would handle the situation myself. Pat Curran and George Hanson, two good reporters and old friends, walked in. They were friendly and a little sympathetic, so we chatted for a while and then they left.

I had to have a police escort to get from the dressing room to the team bus. It was the first time I ever experienced anything like that, but what else could I expect from the Montreal fans?

They were pretty abusive as I walked through the crowd. Then I spotted some members of the Rangers fan club who had made the trip to Montreal. They kept yelling things like, "We're all for you, Vic," and "Don't listen to these bums . . . they're all crumb bums," and I broke out laughing. It was the only time I laughed in Montreal the whole night.

OCTOBER 16

It's Monday afternoon and I've already forgotten about the Montreal incident. Well, almost. We beat the North Stars, 6–2, last night at Madison Square Garden and I got my first goal of the season. Now all I need is forty-nine more to match my output for last season.

I beat my old roomie, Gump Worsley, during a first-period power play. Ratty passed to me on left wing and I let it go from the face-off circle. Gump sprawled to his right, but was too late. The puck flew just inside the left post and into the net.

As I skated past Worsley, I said, "Thanks, Gump. I needed that." He glared at me and uttered a few unkind words. Nobody in the league can cuss like old Gump.

I'd like to say one more thing here about Worsley. He put in some rough years with the Rangers back in the fifties. He took a lot of abuse from the fans in those days, but he'd shrug it off and never lose his sense of humor.

Gump got off a memorable remark while playing for

23

New York that has grown old with age, but it's worth repeating here. A reporter once asked him what team gave him the most trouble and, without blinking an eye, the Gumper said, "The Rangers, dummy."

Maybe it's because of all the abuse he used to take in New York, but Gump loves to come back and knock off the Rangers. He never had a chance last night. We outshot the North Stars, 44–19. Gene Carr set up a second-period goal by Walt Tkaczuk that proved to be the winner.

At the start of the game, the Garden fans were riding Carr unmercifully. They had watched our game against the Canadiens on TV Saturday night and saw Gene make an obvious mistake. He tried to shoot the puck out of our end and missed it. The miscue led to a Montreal goal. Gene rode the bench for the rest of the night.

Emile decided to give Carr another chance against the North Stars. The Garden fans were riding Gene pretty good until he helped set up Tkaczuk's first goal of the season. Gene broke loose from Bob Nevin, another old buddy, and took a pass from Park on the left side. Gene went in deep and then relayed the puck to Tkaczuk. Walter beat Worsley from low in the slot.

Now the fans were on their feet cheering Carr. When Gene got back to the bench, all the fellows were whacking him on the back. Later, somebody asked him how it felt to hear cheers instead of jeers. Gene laughed and said, "I think I'll run for mayor."

That was a big game for us. Tkaczuk and I both got our first goals of the season. Gilles Villemure made his first start in goal after missing the first four games with his aching wrist and wound up a winner. Steve Vickers got two goals.

Worsley contributed another good line when somebody suggested that on Vickers' second goal the puck appeared to drop about 10 feet. Gump snarled and said, "Yeah, it dropped all right . . . right between my legs."

We still own only two victories in our first five games—not too good. But I could see signs of improvement against the North Stars. We came out hitting, something we hadn't done in our previous games. And we started to play better positional hockey. We had a team meeting before the North Stars' game, and this is what Emile stressed. He decided we'd just send the center in to forecheck, leaving the wingers to pick up their checks. It worked out fine.

OCTOBER 17

Guess who's coming to town? The flippin' Bruins. We play them tomorrow night at the Garden. We've had two tough practices—yesterday and today—to get ready for those busters from Boston.

OCTOBER 19

We were ready. We beat the Bruins, 7–1. They're still playing without Bobby Orr, who had knee surgery during the summer and hasn't recovered yet. Sure, the Bruins miss Orr. But they also miss Gerry Cheevers, who jumped to the WHA. Eddie Johnston can't carry on alone. He and Cheevers used to alternate in goal; now with Cheevers gone, Eddie has a lot of pressure on him. Maybe too much pressure.

Johnston was in goal last night and looked a little frustrated. So did most of the other Bruins. Phil Esposito took four shots and came up empty. He has now played seven straight games against us—six in last spring's play-offs—without scoring a goal. Near the end of the game, Esposito tried to crosscheck Glen Sather. Slats moved out of the way just in time. He used to play with the Bruins, so he knows Phil well. Slats said he was surprised when Phil tried to use his stick on him. "That's not like Phil," he said.

I talked with Esposito and Johnston in the hallway between our dressing rooms before the game. Phil was sympathizing with me over the riding I got in Montreal.

"It's not right the way those fans got on you," he said. "But I guess you knew you were going to receive some abuse, heh. It's too bad it had to happen that way."

Johnston is still bitter about not playing in any of the games against Russia. "Sinden promised to use everybody, but he didn't use me," Eddie said. "Why make promises if you can't keep them?"

It was a pretty rough game—a typical Bruins-Rangers battle. Right after I scored the first goal in the first period, Sather and Fred O'Donnell went at it pretty good. Mike Walton stuck his nose into it and was given a game misconduct. In the second period, Ace Bailey elbowed Gene Carr. Bailey is all elbows. He put Ron Stewart in the hospital with a double fracture of the jaw in the 1972 play-offs.

This time, Bailey didn't get away with it. Carr chased him down ice, jumped him from behind, and wrestled him to the ice. Both have long, bleached blond hair. I told Carr later he should have yanked at Bailey's hair. "I didn't have time," he said.

A funny thing happened in the first period. One of my shots from left wing was deflected into the crowd. It struck the Garden organ, accidentally turning it on. While the organist, Toby Wright, was trying to shut it off, everybody turned to listen to this single weird note coming from the organ. Wright later explained that my shot hit the high-C key on the lower manual and jammed it.

One reporter, Martin Lader of UPI, suggested it sounded like "The Lost Chord."

"Nope," Bob Gockley of the Long Island *Press* said, "That's 'Poor Johnny One Note.'"

Funny.

We hit the road tonight for a game against the Islanders. Emile Francis is calling it "the shortest road trip on record." And it is. The distance from our homes in Long Beach and Atlantic Beach on the south shore of Long Island to the Islanders' rink in Nassau Coliseum in Hempstead is approximately ten miles. It should take us less than twenty minutes to drive there. That's fifteen miles and thirty minutes shorter than our trips to Madison Square Garden for our home games.

The Islanders are expecting their first sellout crowd for the game. I guess a lot of people want to sit in on history. It will be the first meeting between two New York teams in a regular-season NHL game since March of 1942, when the Rangers and the old Americans were rivals. Don't ask me if I remember the Americans. I was only eighteen months old then.

OCTOBER 23

It was a good weekend. We beat the Islanders, 2–1, Saturday night, then tied the Canadiens, 1–1, at the Garden Sunday night.

The Islanders drew a standing-room-only crowd of 14,665 for Saturday night's game. That was the official count, but I'll bet there were at least 16,000 in Nassau Coliseum. It was a strange crowd, too. There were probably as many Ranger as Islander fans there, so there was lots of cheering for both teams. One fan hung a banner that read: "Let's Go New York!?" He was being very neutral.

The Islanders gave us quite a fight. I broke a scoreless tie in the second period when I beat Billy Smith with a slap shot during a power play. I let it rip from about fifty feet out and got good wood on it. Smith could have been screened on the shot, but he offered no alibi. "I saw it," he said. "I just didn't move fast enough. It banged just inside the post."

Craig Cameron tied it for the Islanders about three minutes later, then Bobby Rousseau won it for us with a third-period goal. You hear a lot of talk in sports these days about second effort. Rousseau got that goal on a third effort. Smith stopped Bobby's first shot. Bobby fanned on the first rebound, then recaptured the puck and put it past Smith.

Smith showed me something in that game. He's quite a fighter. Early in the second period, Smith and Gilbert started shoving each other in front of the Islanders' net. Smith dropped his stick and gloves but not his mask, then started mauling Gilbert. Rod isn't a bad fighter, but he held back this time and some of the fans were hollering "chicken."

This made Rod laugh. Rod said, "I had him [Smith] set up for a sucker punch, then I realized he still had his mask on. There was no way I was going to hit him and not wind up with a busted hand. Why didn't he take his mask off?"

"Why should I?" Smith said. "In an incident like that you don't have time. While I'm unfastening my mask a guy could land a half-dozen punches. Nope. I keep the mask on."

Smith is a tough kid, all right. But one of these days he's going to try roughing up somebody in front of the crease and—mask or no mask—that somebody is going to drop him on the seat of his pants.

Our tie against the Canadiens was a classic goaltending duel—Ken Dryden against Gilles Villemure. Both goals were scored in the second period. Gilbert beat Dryden with

a thirty-footer. A minute later, Marc Tardif banged a rebound shot off Villemure's pads.

Dryden and I have done a little kibbitzing from time to time. He's a big, friendly guy and I like to needle him. I've scored some goals against him, but he's also robbed me a few times. Whenever we're playing Montreal and Dryden stops one of my shots, I'll holler, "Lucky stiff." Kenny will just shake his head, but beneath that mask I'll bet he's grinning.

Dryden, of course, has more than luck going for him. He's a damn good goaltender. And so is Villemure. In that 1–1 tie against Montreal, Gilly didn't panic when Yvan Cournoyer moved in on him on a breakaway. He stood up, blocked Yvan's first shot, and then used his right pad to kick out the rebound. The Garden crowd gave Gilly a standing ovation.

Gilly has the perfect temperament for a goaltender. Nothing ever seems to bother him. We call him "Whitey," because he has a pale complexion. He looks like a guy who has been dipped in a barrel of flour. But he's got a lot of guts—like most goaltenders.

OCTOBER 26

Villemure did it again. He was in goal last night when we beat the Philadelphia Flyers, 6–1. Gilly is now unbeaten in five games (four victories and a tie) since he shook off that wrist injury and took over for Giacomin. In those five games he has given up only six goals. He's really hot.

Gilbert also had a big night against the Flyers. He scored twice and set me up for a goal. We didn't think Rod would be able to play. His right thigh was swollen. He was kneed by Frank Mahovlich in Sunday night's game against Montreal and developed an old-fashioned charley horse.

29

Rod spent the last two days taking treatment. He told me the thigh was bothering him during last night's warmup, but he decided to play anyway. He felt a litle better after getting his 250th career goal in the opening period. I reminded him then that he owed the guys the first round of beers at our next party, to celebrate that milestone. Rod gave me that silly grin and said, "Yeah, sure, I'll buy the first round." Wanna bet? We'll probably end up sharing a can of beer.

But don't knock Rod Gilbert. He's had his share of injuries during his years with the Rangers; but he shakes them off and goes out and does his job. Emile was amazed at the way Rod played last night. The boss said, "Geez, if he plays that way coming off an injury, maybe I'll prescribe a charley horse for some of our guys."

The Cat ought to prescribe a couple of days of rest for all of us. But don't bet on that either.

OCTOBER 27

We've got a four-day break between games—the Black Hawks visit us Sunday—but the Cat has worked our tails off in practice for the past two days. I guess he hasn't forgotten how Chicago knocked us off on the opening weekend of the season, and he doesn't want us to forget either.

Every time we play the Black Hawks, I remember an incident involving Emile and one of his pet superstitions. It was late in the 1970–71 season. Giacomin and Villemure were bidding for the Vezina Trophy—the NHL's top goalie award. Their chief rival was Tony Esposito of the Black Hawks. On this particular night, we played the Black Hawks in Madison Square Garden.

Before the game, Emile went through his usual rituals. He always remains in the room next to our locker room,

smoking cigarettes. As soon as the three-minute warning buzzer sounds, he starts his walk. He stops at the drinking fountain in the corridor, takes a sip of water, and then walks into the dressing room.

I sit by the entrance door, and that door must remain open until the Cat closes it. When he enters the room, he makes an inspection tour. If he spots anything on the floor—cotton, tape, chewing gum wrapper, etc.—he picks it up and deposits it in the trash can. He circles the entire room, walks past me, and shuts the door. That's when we receive our last-minute instructions.

Most of the guys were uptight before our game against Chicago. They knew what the Vezina meant to Gilly and Eddie and to the team, too. I could sense the tightness in the room, so I decided to loosen things up.

While Emile was next door, smoking another Lucky Strike, I got a piece of string and tied it to a roll of tape and placed the tape in the middle of the room. I held the other end of the string in my hand. It was light and barely visible on the wall-to-wall carpeting that covers our dressing room floor.

The three-minute buzzer sounded, and in walked the Cat. He spotted the roll of tape immediately and went to pick it up. I gave the string a little tug and the tape moved. Emile tried picking it up again and I gave it another tug. He looked around the room and all the guys were grinning. "Wise guys," Emile said. Then he started laughing.

That was just what we needed to relieve the pressure. We went out and beat the Hawks and helped Gilly and Eddie wrap up the Vezina Trophy.

I wonder what would have happened if the Hawks played a gag like that on their coach, Billy Reay. It probably wouldn't have worked because Reay doesn't have a sense of humor like the Cat.

Gary Smith is the tallest goaltender in the NHL at six feet, four inches. But he was feeling pretty small last night after we beat him and the Black Hawks, 7–1. Wow! Did our line roll. We wound up with ten points—a good night's work. Ratty had two goals and two assists, Rod had four assists, and I had a goal and an assist.

Villemure worked his sixth straight game, and he's still unbeaten. He missed a shutout when old Chico Maki beat him in the third period. Cliff Koroll roughed up Villemure in the second period, and Curt Bennett rode to Gilly's rescue. He hammered the hell out of Koroll behind our net. Koroll left the ice with blood oozing from a cut on his left cheek. If it had been a pro fight, Curt would have been awarded a technical knockout.

This kid Bennett is something extra. He is an Ivy Leaguer, a graduate of Brown University, and he majored in Russian studies. Ask him to say something in Russian and he'll grin and say, "*Nyet*." Too bad I didn't have him with me in Moscow.

Curt is the son of an old goaltender—Harvey Bennett—who had a cup of coffee with the Bruins in the forties and later played with Providence in the American League. Curt is big—about six feet, three inches and 195 pounds. I had heard he could throw punches pretty good and was a karate expert. But this was the first time I saw the kid in action. If I ever get into trouble—on or off the ice—I want this boy on my side.

When somebody asked Bennett about his fight with Koroll, Curt said his father had always taught him to act fast whenever his team's goalie got into a hassle. "It was just reflex action," Curt said. "I saw Koroll and Villemure collide, then it looked as if Koroll was going to punch

Gilly. I skated over there fast and I pushed Koroll but with the intent to commit bodily assault."

Spoken like a true Ivy Leaguer.

OCTOBER 31

The Cat finally gave us a day off yesterday. What a welcome relief. Ever since the start of the season we've had little time to unwind and catch our collective breaths. I think we all benefited from the day off because we had a lot of pep at practice today. We take off later this afternoon for Chicago and a rematch with the Black Hawks. They'll be laying for us, I'm sure, in their own rink.

NOVEMBER 1

We had a team meeting in Chicago Stadium this morning. What did we discuss? No big secrets. The ice surface here is smaller than in Madison Square Garden, so we know we'll have to do closer checking. The Hawks will probably come out fast tonight and try to run at us. We'll have to forecheck them in their own end and be more aggressive.

I talked to Dennis Hull at the rink. Most of the Hawks were there, checking their skates and sticks. I kidded Dennis about whether his sticks had been checked recently.

"It looks like some of the sticks you've been using have quite a hook on them," I said. "Don't you know you're only allowed a half-inch curvature in the blade these days?"

Dennis chuckled and said, "Listen, Vic, the way you guys hammered us in New York you ought to let us use some of those sticks with the old banana blades."

The Hawks came out flying, all right. They outshot us 17–5 in the first period last night, but Villemure was great. He fanned on only one shot—by Chico Maki—then we

33

popped three behind Tony Esposito in the second period. I got the third, and it proved to be the winner. The score: Rangers 3, Black Hawks 2.

I also had a breakaway on Esposito and should have had a second goal, but I messed it up. Tony has a style that you might call knock-kneed. He sometimes gives you quite a hole to shoot at between his pads. On my breakaway, instead of trying to pick a corner, I tried to shoot the puck between his legs. But he closed his legs at the last minute and my shot struck his pads and bounced away. Lucky stiff!

The Chicago fans didn't like Carr's long hair. Every time he stepped on the ice, they whistled at him and yelled things like, "Hey, Blondie, why don't you get a haircut?" Gene pretends that the catcalls don't bother him, but I'm sure they upset him a little bit.

NOVEMBER 4

The Penguins beat us, 6–4, tonight at Pittsburgh. It was Villemure's first loss in eight games. I guess the law of averages was working against him. What hurt, though, was the way we lost. We had a 4–1 lead after twelve minutes, then let them off the hook. We just gave it away like an early Christmas present.

My right thumb is puffed up and hurts like hell. I hurt it in a fight with Bryan Watson. I had just passed the puck, and he sneaked in behind me and tried to give me a cheap shot. He's good at that. But I saw him coming and ducked out of the way.

I was teed off because Watson is always yapping and running at guys from behind. So when the play came back into our end I looked for the pest, found him, and used a little wood on him. We dropped our gloves and I hit him a shot in the head. He's got a real cement head. As soon as we

34

were separated and I got a look at my thumb I knew there was trouble ahead. I hope I didn't break anything.

NOVEMBER 5

That damn Watson. My whole right hand is swollen, but most of the pain is concentrated in the thumb. I still don't know if anything is broken. We flew into Philadelphia early this morning from Pittsburgh and checked into a motel near the Philly airport. I was up at 11:00 A.M. Park was still sleeping, so I left him in the room and went to the motel's coffee shop. When I returned to the room, Brad was up, but I still didn't mention the aching thumb to him. We have a game against the Flyers tonight and I'd like to play.

NOVEMBER 6

We beat the Flyers, 3–2, last night. I watched the game from the press box. I tested my aching thumb during the pregame warmup, and it was no dice. I couldn't hold the stick and I couldn't shoot, so I decided to sit this one out.

On the bus ride up the New Jersey Turnpike, I almost forgot about the thumb. We had some fried chicken and beer and a few laughs. It wasn't a long bus ride—a little over two hours—but it gave the guys a chance to unwind a little bit and shoot the breeze.

I spent most of the day soaking my right hand. I was afraid to visit the doctor because I feared the thumb was broken. I finally went to see Dr. Leibler this afternoon and had the hand X-rayed. The wet plates showed no broken bones. Thank God for that.

NOVEMBER 9

We opened a four-game home stand last night, beating the Vancouver Canucks, 5–2. My right hand still wasn't 100 percent. I couldn't grip the the stick properly, but I played. Walt Tkaczuk scored two goals. He played a typically aggressive game. He and Bill Fairbairn killed off quite a few penalties.

Somebody asked Vic Stasiuk, the Canucks' coach, to compare Tkaczuk and Fairbairn with some of the NHL's old penalty-killers. Stasiuk said, "Those two are good, but I don't know if they're the best who ever came down the pike. When I was with the Bruins we had two good ones in Jerry Toppazzini and Fleming Mackell. And don't forget Gordie Howe and Ted Lindsay. They did a lot of penalty killing with the Red Wings."

What is it about old-timers like Stasiuk? They always seem reluctant to give the modern guys credit and keep harking back to the old days. I wonder if I'll be like that when I'm old and gray. I hope not.

NOVEMBER 13

Talk about aches and pains. Now I have a badly bruised right shoulder. I guess you could say I'm all buggered up.

I hurt the shoulder when I was crosschecked from behind by Walt McKechnie of the Seals in a game at the Garden Saturday afternoon. It happened in the first period. I scored a goal in that period, but later I could feel the shoulder stiffening up and getting worse. I was sure then it was broken or separated or something.

After the game I had Dr. Leibler look at it. He suggested I have it X-rayed, but I talked him out of it. Myrna had brought the kids to the game—they like those matinee games—and I didn't want them hanging around while I went for X-rays. So we went home together, but I had a little trouble hiding the pain in that darn shoulder.

Because of the pain, I didn't sleep well Saturday night. I drove back into the city on Sunday morning for treatment. By this time I couldn't move my right arm. There was no way I was going to play that night against the Kings. I finally had the shoulder X-rayed and they showed no break, no separation. Something is wrong, though, and it worries me.

It was a good weekend for the club—if not for me. We beat the Seals, 7–2, in that Saturday afternoon game, then whipped the Kings, 5–1, Sunday night. A funny thing happened in Saturday's game: Slats Sather scored a goal. It was his first of the season. When Slats walked into the dressing room for Sunday's game, there was a horseshoe wreath of flowers waiting for him. The special cops at the Garden had chipped in to buy it for Slats. He's the cops' favorite player—maybe because he's so wacky.

Teddy Irvine, filling in for me on the Ratelle line, scored in the first minute of Sunday night's game. You could see I was missed. But the real hero was Steve Vickers, with three goals. He now has seven in fourteen games, making him the top goal-scorer among the league's rookies.

We call Vickers "Sarge." It started during training camp when he showed up one day wearing an Army shirt with three stripes on the sleeves. Brad, though, calls him "Pokey." I guess that's because Steve sort of pokes along and talks slow and soft. Off the ice, that is. On the ice, this kid is no slowpoke. And he has some kind of shot.

During Sunday's game, I spent most of my time in the television booth. I ran into Bill Jennings, the president of our club, afterward and he started kidding me. He said, "Vic, we're paying you too much money to sit in the TV booth. You'd better get well in a hurry and get back on the ice."

I hope he was kidding.

NOVEMBER 14

My shoulder felt a little better at practice today. I thought I would be out a couple of weeks, but I've regained the

37

movement in my right arm. Maybe I'll be ready for to-morrow night's game against the Flyers at the Garden.

When we showed up for practice we learned Ron Stew-art had been sold to the Islanders. I guess Ron didn't know whether to laugh or cry. He wasn't getting much ice time with us, being used mainly to kill penalties, and this is a guy who loves to play. I'm sure the Islanders will work his ass off, but it must hurt going from a strong club like the Rangers to an expansion team like the Islanders.

While driving back from practice with Slats and Bruce we stopped at a traffic light in Long Beach, and who pulls up alongside us but Stewie. We all wished him good luck, and Slats reminded him that the Islanders have a rule about their players living in Long Beach. They don't want them fraternizing with us Rangers.

"Guess you'll have to move out of Long Beach now, Stewie," Slats said.

"Like hell," Stewie shouted back. "I got a special dis-pensation to stay here."

I'll bet he has, too.

NOVEMBER 16

My roomie is back on crutches. Brad suffered sprained ligaments in his right knee in last night's game against the Flyers. It happened in the first period. He had just taken a slap shot and was cutting through the left face-off circle when he was blind-sided by Joe Watson. As I went to help Brad off the ice, he turned to me and said, "Vic, the knee is gone."

Poor Brad. He was off to such a great start this season. He's leading all defensemen in scoring, and now this has to happen to him. The doctors estimate he'll be out from four to six weeks. It's a big blow to him and the club.

We beat the Flyers, 7–3, pouring in four goals in the final

period. I was able to play the entire game and set up the winner by Gilbert. And how about that Vickers? He got three more goals. It was the first time in NHL history a player scored hat tricks in consecutive games.

Vickers' accomplishment amazed Sather. Slats said, "I've been in this league for six years and never got a hat trick. This kid comes along and gets two of 'em in two games. What the hell's going on here?"

You can't beat talent, Slats.

NOVEMBER 17

I gave my shoulder a good test today. I stayed on the ice after practice and kept firing pucks at an empty net. There's still some pain in the shoulder, but it felt stong enough for me to consider playing this weekend. We play the Blues at St. Louis Saturday night and the Penguins at home Sunday night.

Gordie Howe showed up at a press luncheon in New York the other day and was asked about my leaving Team Canada. He claimed I shouldn't have left Moscow because I was representing my country and should have stuck it out.

Gordie surprised me. He was acting like a lot of other people—voicing his opinion without knowing the full facts. He should keep his opinions to himself. And who is he to talk? He once ran out on his own teammates in Detroit.

During one of Gordie's last seasons with the Red Wings, they had a sticky situation on the club. Ned Harkness had taken over as coach, and the players were grumbling about some of his rules. They drew up a petition of their grievances against Harkness and everybody signed it, including Howe. Later he had his name scratched from the list.

39

The Detroit players again suggested Gordie try to reason with Harkness. They were looking for help and leadership, but Gordie failed them. He didn't want to get involved.

NOVEMBER 20

We lost two more players during the weekend. Ab DeMarco, who had been filling in for Park, wound up in a St. Louis hospital Saturday night with kidney damage. And last night, Steve Vickers, who had been playing such great hockey, suffered sprained ligaments in his left knee against the Penguins.

We're running out of bodies. Bruce MacGregor's right knee flared up on him in St. Louis and he had to quit. And my right shoulder is giving me more trouble. I felt it pop when I took my first shot during the warmup in St. Louis. I tried to play, but had to head for the dressing room after my first shift on the ice. My entire shoulder and arm felt dead. I had it packed in ice, took more treatment yesterday, and sat out last night's game.

I have now missed four games. That's four more than I missed all last season. It's getting a little disheartening.

DeMarco suffered his injury when he was crosschecked from behind by Garry Unger. It was a vicious attack by Unger and it surprised all of us because Garry isn't usually a dirty player. I guess he was just following instructions. Before the game, I had a little chat with Jack Egers, who used to play for us. He said Sid Abel, the Blues' general manager, wasn't pleased with the way things had been going and told the players they would have to be more aggressive "or else."

Unger, though, was too damn aggressive. The videotape replay clearly showed him jumping DeMarco from behind. It was a real cheap shot, and Garry didn't even get a penalty. The doctors thought they might have to operate on

Ab because blood had been showing up in his urine. But he was feeling much better today and might be discharged from the hospital tomorrow.

Vickers will be out for at least four weeks, maybe six weeks. He hurt the knee when he was tripped by Darryl Edestrand of the Penguins with only three minutes left in last night's game.

It's going to be tough trying to catch Montreal now with so many guys out of the lineup. We could have cut the Canadiens' lead to three points by beating the Penguins, but we didn't. They got some hot goaltending from Jim Rutherford and won, 5–3.

In his postgame interview, Emile said, "I've never seen so many bad things happen to us all at once."

Let's hope they don't get worse before they get better.

NOVEMBER 21

So this is Dixie. We checked into Atlanta today for our first game ever in the Deep South. We play Boom Boom Geoffrion's Atlanta Flames tomorrow night. It figures to be a historic game. Rod, Ratty, and I had dinner in the hotel's dining room. They have a great jazz group appearing there. We listened to the music for a while and hit the sack early.

I don't know if my shoulder will permit me to play against the Flames. It keeps popping out of its socket, and I must admit I'm concerned.

NOVEMBER 22

The shoulder felt a little better tonight and I was able to play. We beat the Flames, 3–1. I got an assist on a goal by Ratty, and this helped cheer me up.

Atlanta was everything we expected. It's a beautiful city,

very clean. The Omni, the home of the Flames, is one of the nicest buildings in the league.

Geoffrion really has his club hustling. He's changed from the days when he coached us. At that time—in 1968 —he was a rookie coach who had played with a lot of us guys. He didn't gain the respect of some—and this hurt him and his coaching. You can see he has the respect of the Atlanta players; they are working their butts off for the Boomer.

In the dressing room after tonight's game Pete Stemkowski went looking for some mouthwash. He pulled a bottle out of trainer Frank Paice's medicine bag, thought it was Listerine, and took a big swallow. Then he let out a scream and spit out a mouthful of tape remover fluid.

Poor Pete got no sympathy from the gang.

"What a Polish joke you are," somebody yelled.

When I stopped laughing, I shouted, "Hey, Pete, what was that stuff you were drinking—a new kind of Polish mouthwash?"

Even Pete was laughing by this time.

NOVEMBER 24

We had nothing to be thankful for on Thanksgiving. We played the Sabres at Buffalo and lost a toughie. I scored a goal in the third period to put us ahead, 3–2, and it looked like we had the Sabres on the ropes. But they stormed back with three goals against Giacomin to beat us, 5–3.

It was one of our most discouraging losses. We're shooting for first place and can't afford to blow leads like that. I felt sorry for Giacomin. Those five goals weren't all his fault. We let him down terribly by playing sloppy hockey.

I phoned Andy Bathgate before leaving Buffalo to check on the progress of our new golf course. Andy wasn't home. His wife, Merle, told me Andy got three goals in one of those Old-Timers games in Toronto the other night. I said, "Merle, you're going to have to start another scrapbook for that guy." She giggled and said, "Hey, maybe you're right."

Andy was some right wing in his days with the Rangers and later with the Maple Leafs and Red Wings. Too bad he retired. We could use him now with so many guys on the injured list.

Bruce and Audrey MacGregor joined us in a delayed Thanksgiving celebration at our house tonight. Plenty of wine on the table, good food, good conversation.

Our next game is Sunday night against the Maple Leafs. I have something to prove against those guys, so I'm going to give it all I have. The hell with the shoulder. I really want to stick it down their throats and the throats of the Toronto fans.

NOVEMBER 27

O, what sweet revenge. We creamed Toronto, 7–4. I got my ninth goal and drew an assist on Ratty's ninth of the season. The two points gave me a career total of 476, so now I'm tied with Camille Henry for fourth place on the Rangers' all-time scoring list.

Stemkowski had a big night. He took over Vickers' left-wing spot on the Tkaczuk line and got two goals. Maybe Pete should have another swig of that new Polish mouthwash.

I could sense a good game ahead while driving to the Garden with the fellows last night. We have Neilson, MacGregor, and Sather in our car pool. It was my turn to drive. It's always my turn to drive. Anyway, we did a lot of joking around on the trip from Long Beach. Everybody felt real loose.

Even Neilson was yakking it up, which was unusual.

He's normally very quiet before a game. Slats was kidding Bruce about all the sleep he gets. Bruce likes to take those quickie naps—after practice, before a game, before and after dinner. He fights his wife, Audrey, for the couch at his house.

Slats said, "You look like you just got up from a nap, Brucie. What did you do? Kick Audrey off the couch again?"

"You better believe it," Bruce said.

After the game, Dan Proudfoot, one of the Toronto writers, came into our dressing room. He had cut me up pretty good in his paper after I left Team Canada, so I was laying for him.

"Hey, Proudfoot, you've got a lot of guts walking in here," I said.

He started stammering about how he didn't learn the real reason for my leaving until later. I interrupted him and said, "So you wrote all that crap anyway, huh. Thanks a lot. That really did me a lot of good. Now get the hell out of here."

I used to think Dan Proudfoot was a friend of mine, but no more. With friends like that, who needs enemies?

We had a birthday party for Neilson after the game. It was held at Duff's in Greenwich Village. All the players and their wives were there and everybody had a good time, especially the birthday boy. The Chief always enjoys himself at parties.

NOVEMBER 28

Want to take a trip? Come with us on a typical flight to Vancouver. We checked into the Hotel Vancouver tonight after spending 7½ hours on the plane. What a drag. Some of the guys spent their time on the plane playing chess. It's replacing card playing as our favorite game. I don't understand the game, but Sather thinks he's the champ. He lost again. His next victory will be his first.

Brad Park joined us on the trip out here, though he won't be ready to play for another month. He's probably been getting a little restless sitting at home, watching TV and ordering his wonderful wife, Gerry, around. I told him he made the trip to save his marriage, but I was only kidding.

We play the Canucks tomorrow night. It will be my first game here since the Team Canada incident, and I don't know what to expect from the Vancouver fans. Will they boo me? A lady called me after we checked in and said to ignore the fans if they start booing. "They even boo their own players here," she said, "so don't let it disturb you. You have a lot of people on your side around here."

NOVEMBER 29

The Canucks beat us, 2–1. It was unbelievable the way we played. We were horrible. It was like a game back at training camp before the guys get into condition—real sloppy. The only solace I got out of it was the absence of booing. I wasn't exposed to a bit of criticism while I was in Vancouver, and that was a relief.

We arrived in Los Angeles at three this morning for a game against the Kings tonight. Two games in two nights on a trip like this is murder. The time changes and the different weather and all the traveling can leave you weary.

Curt Bennett wasn't with us on the flight from Vancouver. He's been traded to Atlanta for Ron Harris, a veteran defenseman. I like Curt. He's a real conscientious kid with a good head on his shoulders. He wants to be a lawyer or a diplomat in the foreign service some day.

I don't think Curt was happy taking occasional shifts on defense for us. He'd rather play up front. But he rushed the puck too much on defense and made some mental mistakes.

45

With Park out and DeMarco just getting over his kidney injury, Emile wanted a more experienced defenseman. Harris fills the bill. I'm sure Emile hated to give up a promising kid like Bennett, but I suppose that was the only way he could get Harris.

NOVEMBER 30

The Chief bit the dust last night. After our 2–2 tie against the Kings we learned Neilson broke a bone in his right foot while trying to block a shot. What a bloody coincidence. In an exhibition game against the Bruins in September he suffered a similar injury. This time it was the same foot but a different bone.

There's no telling how long the Chief will be out. It's a good thing Emile got Ron Harris from Atlanta. He was pressed into service right away as Neilson's replacement. For further protection, Lawrence Sacharuk has been called up from Providence of the American League. He's a thick-necked defenseman who was playing amateur hockey in Saskatoon at this time last season. He was a fifty-goal scorer out West, which is pretty good shooting for a defenseman in any league.

But what we need now is defensemen who know how to stop goals from being scored against us. The loss of Neilson and Park has put a tremendous amount of pressure on Rod Seiling and Dale Rolfe—our only remaining regulars on the backline.

The boss can't believe what has been happening to us in the way of injuries. We were chatting after the Kings' game and Emile said, "Do you know since training camp we have had our full squad together for only one game?" He's right, too. I looked at our list of injuries that Frank Paice keeps in a little black book the other day, and it's frightening.

There's no rest for the wicked. We completed our three-games-in-four-nights tour of the West last night by settling for a 3–3 tie against the Golden Seals at Oakland. We flew back across the country today and have to play the Atlanta Flames at the Garden tomorrow night.

Our first trip of the season to the Coast wasn't too profitable. Two ties and a loss. Those ties bug me. Still, I feel our line played one of its better games against the Seals. We were getting two men on the puck, something we hadn't been doing in the past. I picked up my tenth goal by beating Gilles Meloche in the first period.

My shoulder seems to be getting better with each passing day, but my left knee puffs up on occasions. The pain is as persistent and aggravating as a toothache, and I find myself favoring the knee quite a bit. I'm not able to make those quick stops, turn, and get rolling again. I find myself coasting sometimes, and that's not the proper way to skate—or play. But with so many guys on the injury list I don't want to take any time off now, though I could use a rest.

The boss pulled a new one on us yesterday. Here we are just back from a weary road trip, trying to catch our collective breaths, and Emile orders a practice for ten-thirty on a Sunday morning. I thought I had seen and heard everything in my years with the Rangers, but this was the first time I could remember practicing on the day of a game. However, I couldn't blame the Cat for working us so hard after the way we played on the Coast. It's a wonder he hadn't done it before.

We really worked, too. We went through our whole practice routine for a good sixty minutes. We had line rushes . . . three-on-two drills . . . then a forward going one-on-one against a defenseman, etc. Plenty of skating and plenty of shooting.

After the drill, we went over to the Penn Garden Hotel for our pregame steak and an afternoon nap. We were really growling by the time we returned to the Garden at five-thirty last night to play the Flames. I don't know if that extra practice was a factor or not, but we won the game, 3–2.

Rod Gilbert scored the winner with a little more than two minutes left to play. We are always kidding Rod about his backhander and how it's so weak he couldn't break a pane of glass with it. But guess how he beat Atlanta goaltender Dan Bouchard? With a backhander.

Emile lost his cool in the final minute when the referee, Bryan Lewis, disallowed a shot by Pete Stemkowski into an empty net. One of the linesmen ruled Stemmer was offside on the play, but none of the officials saw Pat Quinn leave the Atlanta bench and try to intercept Stemmer. That gave the Flames seven skaters—one too many.

Emile drew an automatic two-hundred-dollar fine when he ran onto the ice to protest Lewis' decision. At the end of the game, instead of following us into the dressing room, Emile dashed through a corridor and went looking for Lewis. He found the referee before he reached the officials' dressing room and really tore into him. Emile might have punched Lewis if Boom Boom Geoffrion wasn't there. The Boomer threw his arms around Emile, picked him up, and carted him off.

Our coach might be small, but he's one helluva scrapper.

DECEMBER 5

It was back to work today. We had a rare day off yesterday and I spent it at home, doing a little painting and wallpapering. Our house is in Atlantic Beach, a couple of miles west of Long Beach, where we used to live during the season. I got tired of renting other people's houses, so I bought this place last spring.

It's a large, two-story house near the ocean. It has six bedrooms and a tremendous living room and dining room. We've already made some changes, rebuilding the kitchen and the staircase, and most of the rooms now have wall-to-wall carpeting. I'll rent the house during the summer when we go back home to Oakville.

DECEMBER 8

Would you believe we lost another defenseman last night? Dale Rolfe complained of feeling weak and a little dizzy when we went to the dressing room after the first period of our game against the Buffalo Sabres. He tried to come back late in the second period, took one shift, and then went back to the dressing room.

Goat—that's our nickname for Rolfe—looked worried after the game. "I don't know what's wrong," he said. "My vision got fouled up in the first period and I couldn't see the puck. The doc tells me it might be high blood pressure."

First it was Park, then Neilson, and now Rolfe. Rod Seiling is the only regular among our defensemen who has stayed healthy. He'd better not walk under a ladder or let any black cats cross his path. We need him.

We also need a victory. The Sabres beat us, 3–2. We've only won one of our last five games and three of our last nine. Hurry back, Brad and Chief and Goat. Our defense is really hurting. The whole club is hurting.

DECEMBER 9

Rolfe went through more tests yesterday and they discovered what's ailing him. He suffered a mild concussion

49

about a week ago. It probably happened during one of our games on the West Coast, but Goat wasn't aware of it and kept playing. It finally caught up with him Wednesday night, and that's why he felt so woozy.

He's a tough old goat. He'll probably be out another week, and when he comes back he might have to wear a helmet. There's only one problem there: Where are they going to find a helmet big enough to fit Goat?

We're so desperate for defensemen that Emile used Sather at that position in practice today. You can guess what happened. A puck bounced off Giacomin's pads and struck Slats on the forehead, right between the eyes. He needed twelve stitches to close the wound.

"It's a good thing I turned my head just before I was hit or the puck would have hit me in the mouth," Slats said.

"It's too bad it didn't hit you in the mouth," I said. "Then we wouldn't have to listen to all your bull."

"Yeah," Giacomin said. "What were you playing defense for, anyway? Don't you know that position is jinxed?"

Slats took all the ribbing good-naturedly. He's a great competitor and would play anywhere, even goal, if he thought it would help the club.

DECEMBER 11

Thank God for expansion. Thank God for the Islanders. We played them in a home-and-home weekend series and won both games by 4–1 scores.

Billy Fairbairn helped us win the Saturday night game at Nassau Coliseum with two quick goals. We call him "Dog" because he's so tenacious. Once he gets possession of the puck, he won't give it up—just like a dog with a bone. Billy is also very quiet. Sometimes when you say hello to him he seems to be stuck for an answer. But he's not as shy as he used to be, and he's well liked by all the guys.

50

In our Sunday night game at the Garden, Bill Harris put the Islanders ahead with a first-period goal. Some of the Islander fans have been riding Harris, and this isn't fair. He's only twenty and fresh out of the junior ranks. The Islanders signed him to a big contract—over a hundred thousand dollars a year—and this put a lot of pressure on the kid. The fans expected too much from him.

They should be more patient with Bill. He's big and strong and knows how to handle the puck. There're still a few things he has to learn, like how to throw his weight around and how to get position in front of the net. That will come in time.

Peter McDuffe settled down after giving up Harris' goal and shut out the Islanders the rest of the way. Fairbairn scored before the end of the first period to tie the score, and I got the winner in the second period.

It was McDuffe's first start of the season. He's being carried as the club's third-string goalie behind Giacomin and Villemure. McDuffe would like to be traded to another team so he could play regularly. It's tough on the kid just being a hanger-on, and you can see he's unhappy. He rarely smiles. But that's a good sign. If he wasn't unhappy I'd figure there was something wrong with him . . . that he had no ambition, no desire. He has lots of desire.

DECEMBER 12

After practice today I couldn't help noticing all the people doing Christmas shopping in various department stores on Long Island. It's beginning to feel a lot like Christmas, when folks are supposed to think about peace on earth, goodwill toward men. I wonder if the people in Toronto will display any goodwill toward me when we play the Maple Leafs there tomorrow night?

It will be our first visit to Toronto this season. I used to look forward to this trip. After all, Ontario is my home province. I have many friends in Toronto—and enemies, too.

All I can think of now is having a good game against the Leafs and helping us win. Maybe that's the only way to silence those fans who still feel I was wrong in leaving Team Canada.

DECEMBER 13

It was a wild night in Toronto. We won, 4–3, after blowing a 3–0 lead. I was subjected to some booing and heckling; I got involved in an altercation with a fan after the game, and the bus that was supposed to take us to the airport broke down.

First, the game: Stemkowski set up our first two goals by MacGregor and Sacharuk. It was the first NHL goal for Sacharuk. When Stemkowski scored midway through the second period, it looked like we were home free.

But give the Maple Leafs credit: They didn't quit. They cut our lead to 3–2 before the end of the second period; then Davey Keon tied it at the twelve-minute mark of the final period. They were still fighting like hell when Fairbairn took a pass from Ratelle and beat Ron Low, the Leafs' rookie goalie, with only twenty-nine seconds left to play.

I had three good shots at Low in the second period. One hit the left post and I cursed when it bounced the wrong way. I'm sure I was pressing too hard. I wanted to stick it to those fans who were booing me. The boos started with just a few fans, then others joined in. They were just like bleeping sheep. But it still wasn't as bad as it was in Montreal in October.

The real excitement took place after the game. As we were boarding our bus outside Maple Leaf Gardens, a heckler started riding me pretty good. I told him to get lost, but he kept it up.

Rod Seiling was standing outside the bus, talking to his parents. When Rod left them and came aboard the bus, the heckler started berating Rod's folks. That's when the whole bus emptied. I was in the forefront, along with Park and Sather. We threw the heckler against a wall and told him he'd better beat it. He left in a hurry.

We climbed back aboard the bus, and Emile yelled, "Let's go, driver." But the damn bus wouldn't start. It had a dead battery. We had to wait for the bus company to send us a replacement, so we were an hour late catching our flight to Boston. We didn't check into the Sonesta Hotel until three this morning.

The Sonesta is located in Cambridge, across the Charles River from Boston. I'm sitting in my room now, trying to get psyched up for our game against the Bruins tonight. It's not a hard job for any of us. We're always ready for the Bruins.

DECEMBER 14

How would you like to be a goaltender and have 55 shots fired at you in 60 minutes of hockey? That's the type of barrage Gilles Villemure was subjected to in our game against the Bruins tonight. We lost, 4–2, but it could have been a helluva lot worse if little Gilly hadn't come up with some great saves.

In the first period, the Bruins took 22 shots at Gilly and he stopped every one of them. Even the Boston fans were cheering him at that point. But how much can a guy take? He finally weakened in the second period, and the Bruins scored 4 goals in 5 ½ minutes.

The Boston players weren't gloating, though, at the end of the game. They know it would have been a different story if three of our defensemen—Park, Neilson, and Rolfe —weren't nursing injuries.

Villemure earned one distinction tonight: Phil Esposito took fifteen shots at him without scoring. Phil said, "I couldn't believe some of the saves that little bugger made on me. He was fantastic." You're so right, Phil.

During one of our power plays, I was playing the left point when Bobby Orr picked up a loose puck and started skating toward me. I'm no defenseman, but now I had to act like one. It's Bobby Orr vs. Vic Hadfield, one on one. What do I do now?

As Orr neared me, I hollered, "Okay, Bobby, come on. You don't scare me." He looked up and started to laugh. Then he skated into a corner, still laughing, and took a weak shot that missed the net.

But that wasn't the end of it. Seconds later, Esposito winds up with the puck and now I'm one on one against him. I had been so successful in stopping Orr, I decided to try the same thing on Phil. I yell, Phil laughs, and he winds up taking a soft backhander that Gilly handles easily.

Maybe that's the secret to stopping Orr and Esposito. You have to tickle their funnybone.

DECEMBER 15

Most of our flights are uneventful, but not the one we took today from Boston to Minneapolis. We were about a half hour out of Boston when the commercial jet we were on hit a downdraft. It felt like somebody had pulled a rug out from under us.

A stewardess who was walking up the aisle lost her balance and Gene Carr grabbed her. Gene probably saved her from serious injury because she could have struck her head on the roof of the cabin. "That was the best catch I made all season," Gene said. Damned if it wasn't.

The plane pitched around quite a bit before the pilot

finally regained control. While all this was happening, Bobby Rousseau was saying his prayers. If you think Villemure has a fair complexion, you should have seen Bobby's face. It was pale with fright. But he wasn't the only pale-face. We were all scared.

Later in the flight, Rousseau had calmed down enough to finish one of his latest oil paintings. He's quite an artist—for a hockey player. This particular one depicted an old weather-beaten chapel in Quebec. Tkaczuk grabbed the painting and tried to auction it off.

"What am I bid for this fine work of art?" Walter shouted. "Do I hear fifty dollars? How about twenty-five? No? Somebody make a bid. How about five dollars?"

There were no takers. Then Walter said, "Will somebody pay Bobby two dollars to take it back?"

Everybody chuckled, including Bobby. It helped us forget that hole in the sky our plane had hit an hour earlier.

DECEMBER 17

Save me from any more road trips like we completed last night. We lost to the North Stars, 5–1. Old Gump Worsley of the North Stars, who has been sidelined with a pulled thigh muscle, watched the game from the press box. He turned to a reporter near the end of the game and said, "I've never seen the Rangers skate so poorly . . . they look terrible."

Gump was right. We were terrible. And because of this we couldn't wait to leave Minnesota. Then we ran into more trouble. Our chartered plane was about to leave the terminal when it developed starter trouble.

We lost two hours waiting for the airline to supply another plane and didn't leave Minnesota until 1:00 A.M. (2:00 A.M. New York time). It was 5 A.M. when we checked into the Penn Garden Hotel, and we have to play the Penguins at the Garden tonight.

DECEMBER 18

Home ice, it's wonderful. We beat the Penguins, 9–1, last night, scoring three goals in each period. It was our best offensive game of the season. I was glad to see Gene Carr get his first NHL hat trick. He's taken some abuse from the fans, but he has great desire, and if he keeps digging he's going to be a tremendous hockey player.

How could we have looked so bad against the North Stars, then turn around and play so well against the Penguins after staying up all night? Emile Francis claims he has the answer. "Maybe a 5:00 A.M. curfew is in order from now on," he said.

Bite your tongue, boss.

DECEMBER 19

Dale Rolfe is back and he isn't wearing a helmet. Now if Brad Park and Jim Neilson and Steve Vickers would hurry up and get back into action we might be able to catch those Canadiens, who are three points ahead of us.

We play the Blues at St. Louis tomorrow night. I miss Park, my old roomie, on these trips. We call him "Porky" because he has such a large caboose. I miss him getting up in the middle of the night, slamming doors, banging the toilet seat, and blowing his nose. Yeah, I miss Porky like a hole in the head.

Ted Irvine, my new roomie, is a lot quieter. He's been trying to teach me to play chess, but with little success. Ted doesn't always wear his contact lenses during our lessons so he has trouble seeing the pieces. It's like the blind leading the blind.

56

We lost two more players—Irvine and Carr—while beating the Blues, 5–4, last night. Teddy crashed into the boards—there was nobody near him at the time—and twisted his left knee and ankle. He'll be out from four to six weeks.

Carr fractured his right collarbone when he was checked into the boards by Bob Plager. He was kept overnight at a St. Louis hospital. A doctor there said Gene will be out at least six weeks.

This is getting ridiculous. It's hard to believe that one team can suffer so many injuries in such a short time. We finished last night's game with only fifteen players. "It was the same as our last game here," Emile said. "I ran out of players."

St. Louis has become a jinx town for us. MacGregor and I couldn't finish our last game here in November, and DeMarco wound up in the hospital that night when he was speared by Garry Unger. The Blues are giving us the blues. We're going to have to get even with those guys someday.

Our 5:00 A.M. curfew didn't work this time. We didn't get back from St. Louis until five yesterday morning and showed up at the Garden a little groggy for our game against the Atlanta Flames last night. You guessed it. The Flames beat us, 5–2, and was Boom Boom Geoffrion happy.

The Boomer was standing in a Garden corridor talking to newsmen after the game. He was wearing a checked sports jacket, a polka dot tie, and a smug look. "I never thought we would beat the Rangers in our first year," he said. "I

57

know they have a lot of injuries but, heh, this gives me a real charge, you know."

I'm glad the Boomer was gracious enough to mention our injuries. We now have eight players in the infirmary. And at the end of last night's game, I couldn't see out of my left eye, Gilbert had a bruised knee, and Ratelle was complaining of chest pains.

Ratty and Rod claim they'll be ready for our next game against the Red Wings Sunday. I wish I could say the same. Noel Price, the Atlanta defenseman, and I were fighting for a loose puck in the second period of last night's game when his stick caught me above the left eye.

I'm sure it was an accident, but it left me with a beautiful shiner. I look like I just lost a fifteen-round decision to George Foreman. The eye is completely closed.

DECEMBER 23

I must be a fast healer. I can see out of my left eye today—just in time to greet my parents at the airport. They flew down from Oakville to help us celebrate Christmas. My dad—his name is Vic, too—was making his first plane trip. I kidded him about needing a change of underwear when I met him at the airport. He laughed and said, "Don't be a wise guy."

My mother's name is Noel. She was born on Christmas, so we'll have a double celebration the day after tomorrow.

DECEMBER 25

Joyeux Noël. We beat the Red Wings, 5–0, yesterday afternoon at the Garden and then returned home for a wonderful Christmas Eve with my family. I left a toy car under the Christmas tree for my parents. When they picked it up this morning I explained it was a replica of a car I had ordered for them as a Christmas gift. The real car will be waiting for them to claim when they get home. Mom and Dad were pretty excited about that.

I was excited about our victory over the Red Wings. My eye was okay and I was able to play. I set up a goal by Rod Seiling.

We regained three of our walking wounded—Neilson, Park, and Vickers—another nice Christmas present. Tom Williams and Bill Heindl have been called up from Providence as replacements for Carr and Irvine. Heindl scored a goal against the Red Wings, and wasn't he happy.

DECEMBER 28

We got knifed by the Sabres again. I know that's a play on words, but it's accurate enough. Those bloody Sabres and Dave Dryden, that long drink of water in goal, beat us last night, 4–1.

It was the second straight time Dryden stuck it to us—and at the Garden, no less. He's as big as his brother, Ken, and covers a lot of the net. When Dave came into the league he used to sprawl a lot and get caught out of position. He was easy to beat then. You'd wait for him to slide out, then hit the open man with a pass or flip the puck over him. He stands up more now and is a greatly improved goaltender.

Gil Perreault was all over the ice last night. He set up the Sabres' first goal by Rene Robert and scored the fourth against Gilles Villemure. Brad Park's knee is bothering him. Maybe he was rushed back too soon. He didn't play against the Sabres and may miss our New Year's Eve game against St. Louis.

There was some swelling in my left knee, so I skipped today's practice. Emile shook up our forward lines, switching me and Steve Vickers. The boss wants to try me with

Tkaczuk and Fairbairn. Steve has my old spot on the Ratty line.

We closed out 1972 by beating the Blues, 6–1. Ratty got the hat trick, and Gilbert scored his first goal in twelve games. Late in the game I was sitting next to Ratty on the bench. He was smiling about his three goals and I said, "You guys really miss me, huh." The boss, who was standing behind us, heard my remark and started to laugh.

When Emile makes line changes he does so for the good of the team and can't think about individuals. That's the way it should be. I don't mind playing with Tkaczuk and Fairbairn. If it will help the team, it's okay with me. I'll play all the harder. Our line looked pretty good last night, too. Tkaczuk got a goal and I didn't miss a shift, though the knee is still a little sore.

After the game we had a New Year's Eve party at Gallagher's 33 near the Garden. All the fellows made only one resolution: to stay out of the hospital in '73.

Eddie Giacomin made history last night when he shut out the Los Angeles Kings, 3–0. It was his forty-first shutout as a Ranger, wiping out Davey Kerr's old club record. Glen Sather also had a reason to celebrate. He got the hundredth point of his career when he scored into an empty net in the final minute.

The fellows were needling Slats pretty good after the game.

"Hey, Slats, were the first hundred points the hardest?" Stemkowski shouted.

"Was that my hundredth?" Slats asked. "I didn't even realize it."

"Don't kid us," I said. "That's all you've been thinking about for weeks."

We then reminded Slats that it would be his turn to buy on our next "deli day." Whenever a guy gets a shutout or a hat trick or an historic goal, he has to pop for the beer, sandwiches, and french fries after our next practice.

Eddie also owes us a "deli day" treat for his shutout. He was fantastic against the Kings. He made some key saves early in the game. Rogie Vachon also played well for the Kings. I'll never know why Montreal traded him to Los Angeles. He's always been tough against us.

I set up a goal by Ab DeMarco in the first period. The score remained at 1–0 until the third period when I beat Vachon with a deflection shot during a power play. Then Slats got that empty-net goal and history was made.

JANUARY 7

Joe Crozier, the Buffalo Sabres' coach, was crowing after his club beat us for the fourth time last night. "We're the New York State champs," Joe said. Maybe he's got a right to crow. The Sabres are now 4–0 against us and 3–0 against the Islanders.

Crozier has done a good job with the Sabres since replacing Punch Imlach as coach. I can't pinpoint the real reason for our bad luck against Buffalo. We led, 1–0, after two periods last night on a goal by Vickers. In the third period, the Sabres outshot us, 17–5, and put four goals behind Giacomin to win, 4–1.

We have always been a good third-period club. The Cat claims that's due to our conditioning. We like to think we're in better shape than any team in the league. But the Sabres simply overpowered us in the third period, and that's what bugs me.

Dave was super in goal. He's been a big factor in the way the Sabres have turned things around this season. Buffalo is also getting a lot of goals from guys who normally aren't big scorers. Look at Gerry Meehan. He's already got twenty-four goals. That's five more than he got last year, and the season isn't half over.

Meehan got the crusher last night after Rick Martin broke a 1–1 tie two minutes earlier. Martin's goal was his twenty-seventh. What a kid he is. Rick has a sort of split personality. Before and after a game, you couldn't meet a funnier guy. But during a game, he's very serious-minded. All business.

Give Rick the puck and duck. He's got some shot. Some fellows in the league feel he's too offensive-minded and doesn't do his job on defense. But he figures his main job is to score goals, and he's pretty damn good at that. When he does get lazy on defense and fails to backcheck, he's got Gil Perreault to cover for him.

Perreault has been a great center since he came out of the Juniors in 1970. And the third member of that line, Rene Robert, is an ideal right wing—a good skater with a hard shot. The Buffalo writers have given the line a neat nickname: "The French Connection." All three are French-Canadians. Give them the puck and they'll show you how to connect.

JANUARY 8

Bryan Watson and I had another spat while we were beating Pittsburgh last night. It happened in the first period. I was trying to get position in front of the net when he shoved me and I shoved back. Then we pulled off our gloves and went at it pretty good. In today's paper, one guy wrote that I hit Bryan with six straight rights. He was exaggerating, but I do remember connecting with at least two good punches. I don't know how Bryan feels today, but I feel great, maybe because it helped me get a little revenge. I hurt my right hand in our last fight at Pittsburgh on November 4, and it took me a long time to get over that.

Hugh Delano of the New York *Post* asked me after last night's game why sparks always flew when Watson and I are on the ice at the same time. It wasn't difficult to explain. I said, "We're just two of a kind. Neither of us is the type who backs away from trouble. He's a game little guy, and I have to admire him for that."

However, there's another reason why Watson and I find it difficult to avoid each other. I play the left side and he plays the right side. When I skate down my left wing, Watson is usually there on right defense waiting for me. That's when the sparks fly.

I've had my share of troubles with other guys who play right defense: fellows like Serge Savard, Terry Harper, Bill White, Barry Ashbee, Carol Vadnais, and Barclay Plager. Bobby Orr also plays right defense, but I've never wound up trading punches with him. Some players who have, tell me Bobby can really go.

But so much for the latest Hadfield-Watson boxing match. What I almost forgot to mention was that while I was sitting in the penalty box, Billy Fairbairn started trading punches with Greg Polis of the Penguins. This was another knock-down, drag-out fight.

A funny thing happened while Billy and Polis were being separated. Kenny Schinkel of the Penguins, who hasn't been playing on a regular line, came out on the ice to stretch his legs. He was doing some nifty figure-eights when the referee, Ron Wicks, skated up to Kenny and advised him he was out of the game.

"Are you crazy?" Kenny said. "What for?"

"For leaving the bench during a fight," Wicks said.

"But I didn't get into it," Kenny said. "All I wanted to do was get in a little exercise."

"Too bad," Wicks said. "It's right there in the rule book. I've got to give you a game misconduct penalty."

Schinkel skated off the ice, a little embarrassed and a little poorer. A game misconduct carries an automatic fine of a hundred dollars.

Tkaczuk got a power-play goal for us minutes later, and Giacomin went on to blank the Penguins, 4–0. It was Eddie's third shutout in his last five games. The Italian is playing great goal.

JANUARY 10

Buffalo, Buffalo, what a wonderful town. We checked in here tonight on the first leg of a six-game road trip. This one will make or break us. It's a helluva town to start any kind of trip. I like Gerry Cheevers' line about Buffalo. He once said, "Every time I fly into that city it looks like it had just been hit by an atomic bomb."

At practice this morning back at Skateland on Long Island it was so cold in the dressing room I built a bonfire. I got a couple of two-by-fours and some discarded hockey sticks, placed them in a trashcan, and put a match to them. It got so smoky you could hardly see across the room, but it did take the chill out of the place.

Rod Gilbert missed the team bus that carried us from the Buffalo airport to the Statler-Hilton Hotel. His explanation: "I was talking on the phone to my brother." A likely story.

JANUARY 11

We finally beat the Sabres and that damn Dave Dryden tonight. It's about time. The final score was 4–2. Stem-

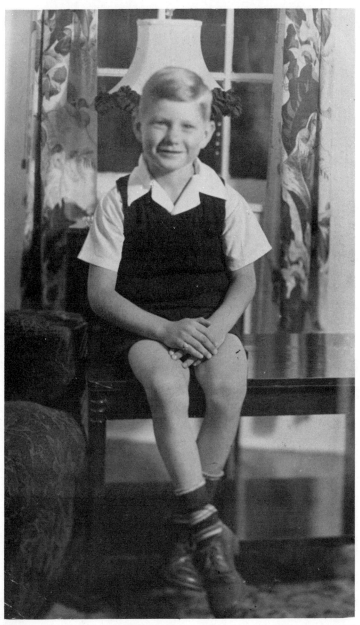

This photo is out of the family album. I was seven years old and, according to my parents, a model youngster. At least that's what they tell me.

Gump Worsley was always tough for me to beat when he was with Montreal. Notice the reaction of the fans behind the net. Gump and I always exchange wisecracks after he makes a save like this . . . (*N. Y. Rangers photo*)

. . . but the little round man can't be lucky all the time. (*Photo by Barton Silverman*)

Tony Esposito of Chicago made a great save on one of my shots in the 1973 play-offs. The puck deflected into the air and flew over the net. That's Rod Gilbert behind me. The other Chicago players are Phil Russell (No. 5) and Doug Jarrett. (*UPI photo*)

This is a good photo of Terry Sawchuk pushing aside one of my shots and Bill Gadsby tying me up so I couldn't chase the rebound. It happened in one of my early (1963) games against Detroit. Sawchuk and Gadsby were tremendous competitors. (*UPI photo*)

My roomie, Brad Park, looks like he's eyeing a girl in the stands. His wife, Gerry, would wring his neck. (*Photo by Paul Bereswill*)

I'm surrounded by Black Hawks but still on my feet. Even Tony Esposito, No. 35, got into the act. (*Photo by Paul Bereswill*)

It was always a thrill playing against Jean Beliveau of the Canadiens. In this 1967 photo, we're searching for the puck in different directions. I wonder who wound up with it? (*Photo by Barton Silverman*)

The secret to winning hockey fights is to land the first punch
... (*Photo by Paul Bereswill*)

... but you can't punch when a linesman gets in the way.
(*Photo by Paul Bereswill*)

How *not* to shoot a slap shot. It looks like I shanked it, doesn't it? Actually, my follow-through is good, but I probably took my eyes off the puck. (*N. Y. Rangers photo*)

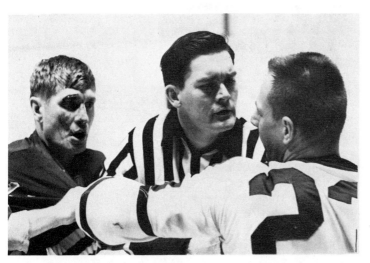

Eddie Shack's hair was short—and so was his temper—when he was playing for Toronto. That's referee Bruce Hood between us. I needed a few stitches over my right eye after this brawl. (*N. Y. Rangers photo*)

The first thing a player drops before a fight is his stick, then his gloves. I also lost my sweater in the 1965 brawl against Montreal. The other identifiable players are Andy Hebenton (No. 17 in dark jersey) and Jean Guy Talbot (No. 17 in white Montreal jersey). (*UPI photo*)

Ron Stewart, the happy fellow behind me, was a witness to this goal I scored against Tony Esposito of Chicago. (*N. Y. Rangers photo*)

Henri Richard, No. 16 of the Canadiens, got so enraged in a 1965 game he skated to our bench to challenge me. That's Phil Goyette to my left and John McKenzie, who later starred for Boston, behind Goyette. (*UPI photo*)

I carried a large chip on my shoulder and kept my stick up early in my career—as this photo proves. The unidentified Detroit player seems to be headed for a fall. (*Photo by Barton Silverman*)

This is one of my favorite photos. I look pretty intense, don't I? (*N. Y. Rangers photo*)

The smiling young man with "Phang" is John Halligan, the Rangers' publicist. He's wacky, too. Most hockey players lose their front teeth, so it's a good idea to have extras. (*N. Y. Rangers photo*)

Another favorite family photo. It was taken during a Rangers Christmas party in 1965. My son Jeffrey was only a toddler then and needed support, but you should see him skate now. A chip off the old block, heh? (*UPI photo*)

Emile Francis and I turn over some extra equipment to Mayor John Lindsay for use by deprived New York children. (*N. Y. Rangers photo*)

Remember when Bobby Orr had a crewcut and he didn't wear No. 4? He was tough to ride off the puck even as a rookie. (*N. Y. Rangers photo*)

It would appear here that I'm ready to conk Jim Dorey, in a game against Toronto in 1971. Actually, I'm just warding off Dorey's attempt to check me against the boards. (*Photo by Barton Silverman*)

Scoring three goals against Tony Esposito in one game isn't easy . . .

. . . so I retrieved the puck on my third goal as a souvenir.
(*N. Y. Rangers photos*)

A day I'll never forget. I needed two goals in our final game of the 1971–72 season to join hockey's elite—and I got them. (*N. Y. Rangers photo*)

The stock photo for a hat trick: three pucks and a borrowed chapeau. I love posing for these shots. (*N. Y. Rangers photo*)

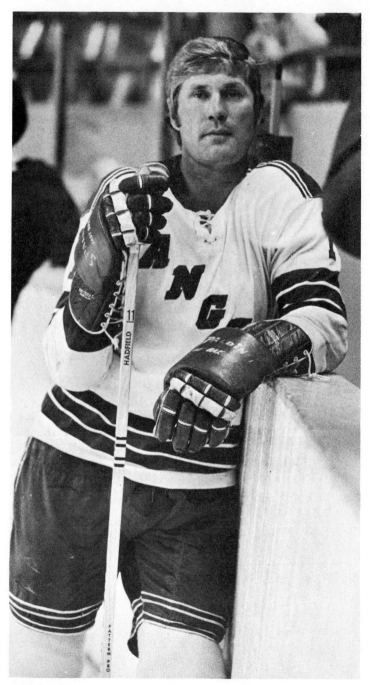

I look teed-off here. That's the look I turn on when Myrna burns the toast at breakfast. Photo was taken at practice. That's Walt Tkaczuk behind me. (*N. Y. Rangers photo*)

kowski got three goals, the third one sailing into an empty net.

Stemmer has been going great guns since throwing away his helmet last month. He claimed it was giving him headaches. Now he's giving the opposition headaches.

The boss put me back on my old line with Ratelle and Gilbert. When we were scoring all those goals last season the writers started calling us the G-A-G Line. It stands for a goal-a-game. None of us are too fond of the nickname, but it is good to be back with Ratty and Rod. Now watch us go—and that's no gag.

JANUARY 12

Everybody keep his fingers crossed. We're back in St. Louis, a real jinx town for us this season. We left Ab De-Marco in a hospital here after our first trip, and Gene Carr wound up in the same hospital with a fractured collarbone on our last visit. That was December 20, and Gene is still sidelined. We can't afford any more injuries.

JANUARY 13

We got out of St. Louis with a 5–3 victory and no injuries. Maybe our luck is turning good.

Bill Fairbairn set up the first two goals by Steve Vickers, then Billy scored on an assist from Steve—all before the end of the first period. But the decisive goal was scored by Glen Sather. Slats now has seven goals, two more than he scored all last season. He's unstoppable.

I met Ted Lindsay before the game and we had a few laughs. He and I had a few scraps when I first came up with the Rangers, but we're old friends now. I wonder if Bryan Watson and I will be old friends someday.

Lindsay was one helluva left winger during his days with the Red Wings and the Black Hawks. He's now trying his hand at broadcasting. He's the color man on the NHL "Game of the Week" telecasts and seems to be doing a good job.

JANUARY 14

This is Super Bowl Sunday. Brad and I are watching the game on television at a motel near the Philadelphia airport. Most of the fellows are rooting for the Dolphins to beat the Redskins. That's because Jim Kiick, Larry Csonka, and Earl Morrall are Ranger fans.

I sent a wire to Kiick before the 1972 Super Bowl game, wishing him luck against the Dallas Cowboys. It didn't help; the Dolphins lost. I was going to send Jim another wire before today's game, but decided against it. I don't want to jinx him.

We play the Flyers tonight at the Spectrum. They beat the Black Hawks at Chicago last night. It was the first time they won a game in Chicago Stadium, so I expect they'll be flying.

JANUARY 15

The Flyers didn't fly too good. We grounded them, 5–2. It was a good day for me. I won a small wager with Brad when the Dolphins beat the Redskins, then got two goals and an assist against the Flyers.

Our line totaled nine points. Ratelle had a goal and three assists, and Gilbert had four assists. I told you the G-A-G Line was ready to roll.

Giacomin played in his seventh straight game. The boss explained he is sticking with Eddie on this trip because "he's real hot." Is he ever. Eddie has given up only twelve goals during that seven-game stretch.

While we were waiting to board our plane at the Philadelphia airport, MacGregor and Sather got into a discussion with Tom Barnwell about goaltenders. Barnwell is an odds-job man with the Rangers and the Knicks. He looks after the equipment, assists the game officials, etc. He's a hard worker, but he has a short fuse.

Barnwell said he was disgusted with an article in a hockey magazine that rated Giacomin no better than thirteenth in a ranking of goaltenders. MacGregor winked at Sather, and the two of them ganged up on Barnwell.

"Giacomin's a good goaltender, but he doesn't belong in the top ten," MacGregor said, winking again at Sather.

Slats went along with the gag. He said, "You're absolutely right, Brucie. Eddie doesn't belong in the top ten."

Barnwell started to fume. "How can you guys talk like that?" he said. "Eddie's your teammate. He's one of the best around."

"Bullshit," said MacGregor.

"Bullshit," said Sather.

Now Barnwell was really burning up. He was ready to fight both Bruce and Slats. Then he caught Slats winking at Bruce and realized they were pulling his leg. Tommy walked away, shaking his head and mumbling under his breath.

JANUARY 16

Remember the Beatles' song, "It's Been a Long Day's Night"? That's the way I feel about the transcontinental trip we just completed. We practiced this morning on Long Island and now I'm sitting in my room at the Sheraton Airport Inn in Los Angeles. It is midnight back in New York.

We were supposed to leave New York at 4:00 P.M. However, there was something wrong with the No. 4 engine on our jet. We sat on the plane for an hour, then had to change to another commercial jet. We didn't leave until 6:00 P.M.—two hours behind schedule.

On most commercial flights, we board the plane ahead of the other passengers and have seats reserved for us in the rear of the plane. We rarely mingle with the regular passengers. But on today's flight, I sat alongside a black soldier from New York who had recently returned from service with the U. S. Army in Vietnam.

I was amazed at some of the things he told me about the war over there. He said he and his Army buddies would go on combat missions and they would have this perimeter to protect and they would stay out there for days on end with little or no rest. While one buddy would try to catch a little shuteye, the other would remain on guard. And there was always the constant fear that if a man on guard fell asleep, their position would be overrun by the enemy. War must be hell, all right.

There was a lot of talk on the plane about Ken Schinkel replacing Red Kelly as coach of the Pittsburgh Penguins. I wasn't surprised. Kenny is a close friend of Tad Potter, who headed the group that bought the Penguins in 1970. Potter had been waiting for the right time to fire Kelly and put Kenny in charge. When the Penguins won only two of their last twelve games, Potter dropped the ax on Kelly.

Kelly sounded pretty bitter about his dismissal. He said, "Some people come into hockey and all of a sudden they think they know everything." That was an obvious dig at Potter. I'm sure, though, that Red won't remain out of hockey too long. He's a good coach.

Schinkel has no coaching experience, so it's going to be interesting to see if he can get more out of the Penguins than Kelly did. When Kenny was a player with the Rangers we used to kid him about his pale complexion and tell him he looked like a life guard in a car wash. He's a quiet fellow, very unassuming, but he's going to have to get tough with some of those guys he was playing with only a week ago.

68

The Penguins made Kenny a winner in his coaching debut by beating the Kings at Pittsburgh Saturday night. We face the Kings here tomorrow night when we resume our six-game road trip. On our last trip out West we picked up only two points on two ties. We've got to do better than that this time.

JANUARY 17

The first twelve players on the East and West All-Star teams have been announced. They were selected by the writers. The remaining eight players on each team will be chosen by the coaches, Tom Johnson for the East and Billy Reay for the West.

Park and Villemure made the East's first team. I'm happy for them, but disappointed that Seiling and Rolfe didn't at least make the second team. They played excellent hockey for us while Park and Neilson were out with injuries. I was also surprised that Tkaczuk and Fairbairn didn't draw more votes. They were the most important guys on our club during the first half of the season.

I wasn't surprised that I was left off the East team. I didn't play well enough during the first half and missed some games with injuries. I finished fourth in the voting among left wingers in the Eastern Division. I don't know who voted for me, but I have a good idea who didn't: the Canadian writers.

JANUARY 18

We got out of Los Angeles with a 4–4 tie after spotting the Kings a 3–0 lead in the first period.

Our defensemen bailed us out. The four goals were scored by Harris, Rolfe, Seiling, and Neilson. Gilbert and I set up the tying goal by Neilson with eighty-two seconds left to play.

69

Gilbert took the puck across the blue line and passed to me. I gave it back to Rod in the right corner and then cut for the slot with Ratty. The Kings' defensemen followed us into the slot, expecting Rod to pass it there. It was the old "sucker" play. Rod then threw the puck across ice to Neilson, who busted in from the left point. The Chief beat Rogie Vachon with a neat wrist shot.

The Chief was pretty happy about his goal. "That's a play we practice all the time," he told the Los Angeles writers.

We were just getting ready to go on the ice at the Forum when Gene Carr walked into the dressing room. He had been in Miami, where he had hoped to bake his shoulder under the Florida sun.

"What the hell are you doing here?" I asked him.

"Aw, it was raining so hard in Florida I decided to come out here and try the California sun," he said.

Gene's not kidding anybody. He was lonesome in Florida and getting itchy to play. He also has a fondness for California girls.

We ran into our Garden cousins, the Knicks, while in Los Angeles. They're on a road trip, too, while an ice show is occupying the Garden. At breakfast in the coffee shop I chatted with Bill Bradley and Dave DeBusschere. I always like to talk to those guys while sitting down because they're so darn tall.

The Seals are our opponents in Oakland tomorrow night. They would like nothing better than to knock us off. They're going nowhere and figure to be real loose.

JANUARY 20

Eddie Giacomin, who had worked the last eight games, finally got a rest last night. Gilles Villemure went back between the pipes and shut out the Seals, 6–0.

70

When Villemure learned he was going to play, he got a little nervous. Gilly hadn't been in a game since December 27.

"I hope I'm not rusty," Gilly said.

Peter McDuffe, who was sitting next to him in the dressing room, mumbled: "If you're rusty, I'm corroding."

McDuffe has worked only one game—that 4–1 victory over the Islanders on December 10. He makes all our trips, but because he's the third-string goalie he watches most of the games from the press box.

Our line totaled eight points against the Seals, and each of us got a goal. Steve Vickers got two more. He's been real hot since shaking off his knee injury.

We took a charter flight out of Oakland and arrived in Vancouver at 2:00 A.M. We have to play the Canucks tonight in one of those early-starting (5:00 P.M.) games, so we're not going to have much time to catch our breaths.

JANUARY 21

Back home at last. We beat the Canucks, 4–2, with another strong comeback. We stayed overnight in Vancouver, left there at nine (local time) this morning, and arrived in Toronto at 5:00 P.M. We then waited an hour for a connecting flight to New York, getting in at about seven-thirty.

It was the best road trip I can remember. We picked up eleven of a possible twelve points, winning five and tying one. Now we're back in the thick of things. We've regained second place from Boston and are five points back of Montreal. See what a little winning streak can do?

That game at Vancouver was a dilly. We were behind, 3–2, early in the third period. Stemkowski tied it and Gilbert won it. On the winning goal, Rolfe fired a long shot from the left point. I deflected it to Rod, and he put it past Bruce Bullock, the Vancouver goalie.

I sat next to Ratelle on the flight from Vancouver. I've known Johnny since our days in the Juniors. He thinks hockey twenty-four hours a day. We talked about how our line is really clicking now, how we help each other by doing a lot of yelling on the ice. Johnny is a quiet man off the ice, but he talks it up pretty good on the ice. I never have any trouble hearing him when he yells, "Hey, Vic, give me the puck," or "Shoot, Vic!"

JANUARY 22

It looks like Harry Sinden and Alan Eagleson picked the remaining players on the All-Star team. Tom Johnson was supposed to choose the final eight for the East team, but I'm sure he got help from Sinden and Eagleson. How else do you explain Gil Perreault and Josh Guèvremont being ignored? They were among the four players who quit Team Canada in Moscow, that's why. I knew there was no way I'd be picked for the All-Star Game, but to bypass Perreault and Guèvremont is ridiculous.

Johnson got caught in a blind switch when John Bucyk, one of his Boston players, begged off playing in the All-Star Game. Johnson was ready then to name Perreault to the East team in order to get off the hot seat, but that would have given him five centers, one too many. Johnson checked Toronto and asked if Dave Keon had already been told he was one of the extra centers named to the team. He had. So Johnson was stuck. He had to ignore Perreault again and pick an extra wing. It wasn't Vic Hadfield.

I attended a reception and dinner at Gallagher's 33 Restaurant tonight. It was given by the Hertz Rent A Car people, who employ me as a sort of goodwill ambassador, salesman, and model. I showed up there with Joe Moderski, director of sports promotion for Hertz, and Frank Olsen, vice president and general manager of the company. They wanted me to meet representatives from some of their biggest accounts. We showed the official film of the 1972 Stanley Cup play-offs. Then I distributed souvenir hockey pucks, signed some autographs, and hustled home. I watched the eleven o'clock news on television and was surprised to learn George Foreman won the world heavyweight championship on a technical knockout over Joe Frazier. What an upset!

JANUARY 23

The big bad Bruins are coming to town tomorrow night. We haven't played them since December 14, when they beat us, 4–2. But we had Park, Neilson, Rolfe, and Vickers out that night. They're all back now and, hopefully, we'll sock it to the Bruins. They're a helluva lot more desperate than we are. They need a victory to tie us for second. If they lose, they drop four points back of us and eleven back of Montreal.

I've heard some rumblings from Boston about dissension in the ranks. The rumors are that if the Bruins don't pull out of their tailspin, Tom Johnson will lose his coaching job. Is Harry Sinden waiting in the wings?

JANUARY 25

The Bruins didn't do much to protect Tom Johnson's job last night. We won, 4–2. Billy Fairbairn scored the winning goal on a great play. Billy and Walt Tkaczuk were killing a penalty to Dale Rolfe in the second period when the puck came loose along the sideboards near center

73

ice. Billy came up with it and he and Walt worked a two-on-one breakaway against Bobby Orr.

Orr drifted slightly toward Tkaczuk, expecting Billy to pass. That was Orr's mistake. Billy faked a pass, then hung a great shot over Ed Johnston's left shoulder. Johnston was amazed by the goal. He said, "That damn Fairbairn. I didn't give him more than an inch to shoot at and he put it over my shoulder. To put it in the corner like that is a helluva play."

Tkaczuk did another great job covering Phil Esposito. He's got Phil talking to himself. Phil has now totaled seventy-seven shots in his last ten games against us and hasn't scored a single goal.

Orr didn't score either. When you can stop Espo and Orr in a game, you've got a good chance of winning.

Brad Park was talking about Orr after the game. Brad said, "Bobby's not skating like he did last year. I don't know if it's because he has to take it easy or he wants to take it easy. Maybe he's worried about that knee acting up again. Right now he's only about 75 percent of the skater he used to be."

I had two assists in last night's game and became the fourth Ranger in history to total five hundred career points. Somebody asked me if I remembered the first point I scored for the Rangers. Hell, no. That was at least fifty years ago.

JANUARY 28

It's Sunday afternoon and Brad and I are in our room at the Penn Garden Hotel watching the Canadiens play the Red Wings on television. We beat the Red Wings at Detroit yesterday afternoon, 6–3, and now we're rooting for them against the Canadiens. A victory for Detroit would

74

give us a big lift for our game against the Maple Leafs tonight at Madison Square Garden.

The Red Wings gave us fits in Detroit. The game was a lot closer than the score indicated. Slats Sather made the picture goal of the game. He took a pass from Jean Ratelle, faked Roy Edwards out of his jock, and backhanded the puck into the net. Slats looked like old Rocket Richard on that one.

Henry Boucha, who is a descendant of the Chippewa Indians, is playing pretty good hockey for Detroit. Every time he stepped on the ice yesterday the organist at Olympia played an Indian war dance. We didn't know if the organist was saluting Boucha or our own Chief, Jim Neilson.

JANUARY 29

The Red Wings did the unexpected. They knocked off the Canadiens in that TV game, 4–2. That provided us with a little extra incentive for our game against the Maple Leafs last night and we took advantage of it. We won, 5–2. We're now unbeaten in ten games and have cut the Canadiens' lead to 5 points.

I got my 20th goal of the season and Jean Ratelle got the 250th of his career. Our line is really rolling now. We totaled 9 points against Toronto. Since I was reunited with Ratty and Gilbert on January 11, we have collected 15 goals and 45 points in 15 games. That's an average of 5 points a game.

John McLellan, the Toronto coach, paid us a nice compliment. He said, "The Ratelle line is the best in the league. Everything seems so automatic with them . . . especially the way they throw the puck around and set up goals."

Red Burnett, who has been covering hockey for the

75

Toronto *Star* since the days of Howie Morenz, dropped by our dressing room after the game and told me the Toronto fans booed Bobby Orr the last time the Bruins played there. I'm not surprised.

The Toronto fans are supposed to be the greatest in pro hockey and now they're even booing a player like Orr. How can they boo excellence? And don't they recognize Bobby's courage? His left knee has to be packed in ice before and after every game. I'm sure the average fan would have trouble walking to the corner drugstore on a knee like that, much less try to play hockey.

I encountered Al Eagleson tonight at the All-Star Game dinner at the Waldorf-Astoria. It was the first time we came face to face since Moscow. He asked me why I was so upset with him.

"It's pretty obvious, Al," I said.

"What do you mean?"

"You know what I mean. You promised you'd meet with the reporters in Moscow and explain my real reason for leaving Team Canada."

"I tried to explain it to them the best way I could," Eagleson said.

I'll bet he did. Needless to say, Al and I are still in Splitsville.

Bob Hope was the principal speaker at the dinner. He got off some pretty good jokes, but the man who really broke up the gathering was Mayor John Lindsay. He's quite a comedian.

Before the dinner I chatted with Bruce Norris, the boss of the Detroit Red Wings. Bruce was telling me about a new pro hockey league he and his associates are forming in Europe. Bruce envisions NHL teams playing regular-season games against the Europeans someday and then meeting in a true World Championship play-off.

Imagine the New York Rangers playing road games in

Sweden, Russia, Finland, Switzerland, England, and France?
I hope it happens before I retire.

The East beat the West, 5–4, in the All-Star Game at the
Garden. It was the first time the game had been held in
New York. Naturally, I would have liked playing in the
game. But what's the use of fretting about it? I stayed
home and watched it on TV with my family.

It was a pretty exciting game. Not too much hitting, but
there never is in these games. Why should a guy go out and
risk injury for $500? That's what they give each guy on
the winning team; the losers get $250. "Give us a little
more bread and you'll see a real All-Star Game," Phil Esposito said. I'm inclined to agree with him.

Gilles Villemure and Eddie Giacomin shared the goaltending for the East. When Giacomin relieved Gilly, midway through the game, the score was tied at 1–1. Eddie
wound up as the winning goalie when Bobby Schmautz of
Vancouver broke a 4–4 tie with about six minutes left to
play.

Greg Polis of Pittsburgh won a new car as the game's
most valuable player. He scored two goals for the West.
And he did it without any sleep. Greg's wife gave birth to
their first child, a boy, in Pittsburgh last night. He stayed
up all night and didn't get to New York until just before
the game. When they gave him the keys to the new car,
Greg said, "I haven't slept for forty-eight hours. And
right now I'm so excited I may not sleep for another forty-
eight." Ah, youth. It's wonderful.

Phil Goyette has been fired as coach of the Islanders. I
guess Phil must have figured it was coming; the Islanders
won only six of their first fifty games. Earl Ingarfield, who
has been serving as a scout for the Islanders, is the new

77

coach. So one former Ranger center is replacing another former Ranger center.

Goyette sounded better when the announcement was made. He said, "I wish Earl luck. . . . He's going to need it." Maybe the Islanders should have given Phil more time— at least until the end of the season. But that's the way it goes in sports; when a team is going bad, they march the coach to the guillotine.

FEBRUARY 1

You have to feel sorry for Gilles Meloche, the skinny young goaltender for the California Golden Seals. We fired fifty-eight shots—almost a shot a minute—at him last night while beating the Seals, 3-1.

A year ago, Meloche was pulled out of a game at the Garden after we pumped nine goals past him. He went to the bench and started weeping. He didn't cry last night, though he had a right to. His defensemen gave him no protection. It must be tough playing goal for a team like the Seals.

Emile Francis, an old goalie himself, admired the way Meloche hung in there. "At least he didn't turn the net around," Emile said. That thought probably never has occurred to the kid.

We used the victory over the Seals to cut Montreal's lead to three points. And we're now eight points ahead of the Bruins, our next opponents. We play them at Boston Saturday night.

FEBRUARY 2

We're running into travel problems even on short hops— like the one we took tonight to Boston. We were supposed to leave from Kennedy Airport, but after waiting around there for an hour we were told our plane was at Newark.

We took a bus to Newark, finally made connections with a flight to Boston, but didn't arrive here until one o'clock in the morning. It was too late to go out to dinner, so we ordered some pizza pies and beer, and sat around shooting the breeze for a while, then hit the sack.

I hope we digest those pizzas before playing the Bruins.

FEBRUARY 3

The pizzas must have given us added strength, or something. We beat the Bruins, 7–3. A big win for us. Any time you beat the Bruins on their home ice you have to feel proud. They came out hitting, but we expected this.

On the Bruins' first rush, Greg Sheppard dropped Park on his ass, then circled the cage and took a run at Vickers. Vickers shoved back and Sheppard skated away with a quizzical look on his face. Sheppard was probably mumbling, "Hey, you guys aren't supposed to hit back." But he picked on the wrong guy when he went after Vickers. Don Marcotte learned the same lesson when he challenged Vickers in the third period. Steve dropped him with a solid right-hand punch. Don Awrey sensed Marcotte was overmatched and went to his rescue. It cost Awrey a game misconduct.

There was another interesting fight between Pete Stemkowski and Ken Hodge. They're both heavyweights. While they were mauling each other, Stemmer kept shoving Hodge toward our bench.

"What were you trying to do, Stemmer?" I asked.

He laughed and said, "It was just like a tag-team wrestling match and I was trying to get to the bench to tag somebody."

"Who were you going to tag?"

79

"The Cat, of course," Stemmer said.

Walt Tkaczuk scored three goals for us. On his last goal, the puck was traveling so fast it went through the back of the net. You don't see that happen very often.

While the linesmen were down on their knees inspecting the net, some joker in the stands yelled, "Leave the hole there and take out Johnston."

The Boston fans jeered Eddie Johnston throughout the game. He got beat on a lot of screen shots and deflections, but the fans don't take that into consideration. They figure every goal is the goaltender's fault.

We were in a frolicking mood after the game. While we were waiting for our plane in Boston, Bobby Rousseau borrowed a woolen hat from an airline mechanic. It was more like a helmet because it covered the ears and had a chinstrap. Bobby put it on and walked around the waiting room looking like an old Kamikaze pilot.

When we arrived at Newark Airport, Ab DeMarco grabbed a wheelchair near our arrival gate. Rod Gilbert jumped aboard and Ab wheeled him toward the main waiting room. In going down an incline, Ab had trouble controlling the wheelchair.

"Put on the brakes, dummy," Rod said.

"This damn thing doesn't have brakes," Ab said.

See what a victory over the Bruins in Boston can do? It makes some guys act like college pranksters.

FEBRUARY 4

Something mysterious is going on here. I stole a newspaper from the Cat while we were waiting for the limousines to take us from Newark Airport to the Penn Garden Hotel last night.

The Cat must have suspected me because as we were leaving the airport the limousine he was riding in pulled up alongside our limousine. He rolled down the window and hollered, "The guy who stole my newspaper had better return it to me when we get to the hotel."

After checking into the Penn Garden, I left the paper in my room and joined the guys for a couple of beers. When I returned to my room, the paper was gone. Did the Cat break into my room to get his damn paper? I can't approach him about it because I would then be exposing myself as a paper thief.

You have to get up early in the morning to outfox the Cat.

FEBRUARY 5

Teddy Irvine is back. He had missed seventeen games since injuring his left knee and ankle against St. Louis December 20. He got a nice ovation when he skated onto the ice in the second period of last night's game against the Atlanta Flames at the Garden. Ten seconds later, Teddy took a pass from Bobby Rousseau and put the puck behind Phil Myre, the Atlanta goalie. One shot, one goal. What a comeback!

I always like to watch Teddy go into that Indian dance of his after he scores a goal. But he didn't do it last night. "I couldn't," he said. "My ankle isn't too strong yet. I was afraid I might fall down."

We turned off the Flames, 6–0. Villemure got the shutout. Stemkowski got another hat trick, his second in twelve games. On his second goal, the puck bounced off Billy Plager, the Atlanta defenseman. It was a fluke, but Stemmer didn't see it that way. "That was a ricochet shot," he said. "Don't forget, I played a lot of pool when I was a kid."

Give the Stemmer credit. He's never at a loss for words.

The Bruins must be getting panicky. They fired Tom Johnson today. Nothing surprising about that. The only surprise was the man who was named to succeed Tom. I figured it would be Harry Sinden, but the job went to Bep Guidolin, who has been coaching the Boston Braves of the American League.

Guidolin is an interesting character. He was the youngest player ever to come into the NHL; he joined the Bruins as a forward at age sixteen. Now he's forty-seven, a tough Italian with a good sense of humor.

When somebody reminded him he was the first Italian coach in the NHL, Guidolin said, "Yeah, the Pope appointed me and he's the only guy who can fire me. He couldn't wait until the end of the season because he heard there's a French Pope coming in and he wanted to make sure one of his own boys made it in the NHL before he packed it in."

The Bruins will have to work their butts off for Guidolin. He made that clear when he took the job. "We've gotta get the bear growling again," he said. "I don't know what it is—complacency, age, money—but instead of growling, we're purring."

I wonder how some of those fat cats on the Bruins will accept a whip-lasher like Guidolin?

FEBRUARY 8

I bumped into Earl Ingarfield before our game against the Islanders at the Garden last night.

"Hey, Earl, I knew you'd make it back to Broadway," I said.

He grinned and admitted it wasn't easy taking over an expansion club, with no previous NHL coaching experience.

"All I hope to do is help make this an exciting club, but I need time," Earl said.

Talking with Ingarfield in the Garden corridor reminded

me of a trick Earl played on Rod Seiling back in 1965. It was Rod's rookie season with the Rangers. We had just returned from training camp in early October and all of us were settled into homes in Long Beach. The weather was great—real Indian summer weather—and Earl suggested we hold a beach party.

Because Seiling was a rookie, he was assigned the job of buying the hamburgers and hot dogs and rolls. He bought enough for about forty people—twenty players and their wives or girlfriends—and then went down to the beach to wait for us.

The party was supposed to start at about seven o'clock that night. At least that's what he told Seiling. But we left poor Rod holding the bag. None of us showed up. Rod ate nothing but hot dogs and hamburgers for the next month and a half.

Ingarfield laughs every time he recalls that incident, but he wasn't laughing after we beat his Islanders, 6–0. We scored three goals against Gerry Desjardins in the first twenty-one minutes, then added three more in the final three minutes. I got the final goal on a power play.

FEBRUARY 10

We're in a wonderful rut. We beat the Islanders again, 6–0. It was our third straight victory by the same score. I got a laugh out of Gilles Villemure after the game. He said, "Jesus, Murphy, isn't that something . . . 6–0, 6–0, 6–0 . . . it sounds like a tennis match."

Gilly was in goal for us tonight. He got all the edge he needed when Bruce MacGregor scored twice during a fifty-second span in the first five minutes. Ingarfield yanked Gerry Desjardins when I scored at 11:40 of the first period.

Desjardins looked a little angry when he went to the bench. He took off his catching glove and flung it into a corner. It was the first time in Gerry's NHL career that he had been relieved in the middle of a period.

"I need more work and I'm not getting it," Gerry said at the end of the game.

Desjardins deserves some sympathy. I've always considered him a good goaltender, but it doesn't matter how good you are if you don't have a decent defense in front of you. And the Islanders' defense is porous, to say the least. Gerry made some good saves against us, but we took so many shots that the law of averages was bound to catch up with him.

We have now won 10 straight and are unbeaten in our last 15 games. And we haven't permitted a goal in 214 minutes and 50 seconds. But after playing the worst team in the NHL in our last two games, we now have to play our next two against a team with the best record in the league: the Montreal Canadiens. We can tie for first if we win the next two.

It should be fun.

FEBRUARY 12

Me and my big mouth. Yesterday afternoon's game against the Canadiens was anything but fun. We blew a 2–0 lead in the third period and had to settle for a 2–2 tie. What's more, Bruce MacGregor broke his left ankle and I broke my right thumb.

Bruce will be out at least a month, maybe longer. He suffered the injury when he was checked into the boards by Guy Lapointe late in the game. I got slashed over the thumb in the first period. I still don't know who the culprit was. I've had so much trouble with that thumb anyway that I ignored it until the third period when I found I couldn't grip my stick properly.

It's strange how one game can turn things around. In our

84

dressing room before the game we were pretty loose. A fan had a picture of the Cat playing goal with Chicago and gave it to Frank Paice. It looked like one of those Gay Nineties pictures. We pinned it to the dressing room blackboard. When the Cat came in and noticed the picture he started laughing. That broke the tension and soon all the guys were laughing.

It was a lot different after the game. We all felt like losers because we knew we had missed a great opportunity to hang one on the Canadiens. Frank Mahovlich snapped our club's shutout streak at 256 minutes when he beat Giacomin early in the third period. We had two players—MacGregor and Tkaczuk—in the penalty box at the time.

Then with about ten minutes left to play, Giacomin came out of his net to stop Lapointe on a breakaway. The puck hit Eddie's stick and bounced to his left. Chuck Lefley picked it up and poked it into the empty net for the tying goal.

I didn't mention my injury to the reporters after the game because I wasn't sure whether the thumb was broken or not. I got the bad news after driving to Lenox Hill Hospital with Bruce and Myrna. Bruce and I left the hospital wearing casts. I climbed back into my car and drove back to Long Island for dinner. Myrna sat in the front seat with me; Bruce stretched out in the back seat. It was a quiet ride.

Later we went to dinner at Al Steiner's in Cedarhurst with Bruce, Glen Sather, and our wives. Emile and Denis Ball were there with their wives. We called Emile over to our table and gave him the news. I thought the Cat was about to get sick.

I said, "Emile, you may as well go back to your table and enjoy your meal. There's nothing you can do now."

He looked at the casts on Bruce's ankle and the cast on my thumb and then looked at his watch. I knew what was going through his mind. He wanted to get to a phone and start calling for help.

FEBRUARY 13

The Cat got some help from Providence. He has called up Jerry Butler, a right winger. The kid isn't too big, but he's wiry and has earned the nickname "Bugsy" in the American League. He also must know where the net is. He has twenty-four goals to his credit.

The Islanders made another deal, shipping Arnie Brown to Atlanta for Ernie Hicke. Brown has already worn three different uniforms this season. I figured this latest trade would upset Arnie, but it didn't. "I couldn't be happier," Arnie said. "At least I'll be playing with a team that has a shot at the play-offs."

Derek Sanderson is back with the Bruins. He claimed the Philadelphia Blazers gve him a million dollars to get out of town. Derek obviously didn't like the Blazers or the World Hockey Association. "Coming back from Philadelphia is like coming back from Vietnam," he said.

The Cleveland Crusaders had approached me about jumping the Rangers last summer. When the Cat heard about it, he sat down and wrote a new three-year contract for me. It was an offer I couldn't refuse. The newspapers estimated my salary at two hundred thousand dollars a year, which was close enough. I can't honestly disclose the actual figure now because of performance bonuses in the contract, but I can tell you I'm damn glad I didn't jump to the WHA.

FEBRUARY 16

The air has gone out of our beautiful balloon. After going unbeaten in sixteen straight games, we lost to the Canadiens at Montreal and to the Sabres at Buffalo on successive nights.

I drove over to Bruce's house to watch the Montreal game on television. Both of us squirmed as the Canadiens won, 6–3. It was more of the same last night. This time Bruce came to my house and we watched the Sabres win, 4–1. Roger Crozier was the difference in that game. The Cat said, "I've seen Roger play some great games in goal, but this was one of his best." No doubt about it.

Crozier has had a lot of trouble with his stomach in recent years. He wound up in a hospital around Christmas and came out about twelve pounds underweight. But he looked awfully strong last night.

I don't think I've ever felt as helpless as I did the past two nights, watching those games on TV. I can't wait for the doctor to cut that cast off my right hand so I can get back into action.

FEBRUARY 19

Ab DeMarco helped pull us out of our tailspin. It was his third-period goal that proved to be the winner last night as we beat the Islanders, 3–2.

Ab stickhandled his way through the Islanders, pulled Gerry Desjardins out of the net, and backhanded the puck in.

I like Ab's style. He hasn't played too much, but when he's on the ice he wants the puck. He knows how to control it and how to shoot. And he's one of the best-skating defensemen in the league. His only problem is a lack of weight. If he could put on about ten or fifteen pounds he'd be a real good one.

Brian Spencer of the Islanders also impressed me last night. When you're playing for a losing club like that, it's easy to get down or lie down. But not Brian. He has played his heart out in every game against us this season.

Gene Carr saw a little action against the Islanders. It was his first game since he broke his right collarbone on December 20. But every time we reclaim one player, we lose another. Park damaged his right kneecap when he threw a hip check at the Islanders' Brian Marchinko in the first period. That finished Brad for the night—and maybe for the next couple of weeks.

FEBRUARY 21

Brad, Bruce, and I—the walking wounded—remained behind when the club took off yesterday for a two-game trip to the West Coast. It's the Kings at Los Angeles tonight and the Golden Seals at Oakland Friday night.

A small earthquake shook Los Angeles this morning. I talked by phone with Pat Doyle, the club secretary, and he told me the tremor rattled windows in the Sheraton Airport Inn, where the team is staying. Pat said our little leader jumped out of bed and lay on the floor. The Cat thought the hotel was going to collapse.

Bobby Rousseau was plenty scared, too. He got out of bed, picked up his clothes, and ran into the corridor. But not Gilles Villemure. He's positively unflappable. He slept through the whole thing.

Pete Stemkowski got off the best crack of the day. He said, "I knew the Cat was going to shake up the team but I didn't think he'd ask God to help him."

Rousseau recovered quickly from the shakes. He made a great play to set up a goal by Ratelle with ten seconds left to play, and we beat the Kings, 4–3. What a comeback. We were trailing, 3–1, in the second period. Billy Fairbairn scored before the end of the second, and Jerry Butler's first NHL goal early in the third tied it at 3–3.

The Kings were hoping to salvage a tie when Rousseau

swept the puck away from Gilles Marotte and headed into the Kings' zone. Bobby sneaked around Harry Howell and fired. Rogie Vachon saved, but Ratelle popped in the rebound.

That was a big two points for us. The Bruins are right on our heels now. They beat the Seals, 6–2, tonight at Oakland.

FEBRUARY 22

A big day for me. Dr. Leibler removed the cast and X-rayed the thumb. The broken bone has started to knit properly. Doc said I can play if I keep the thumb taped.

While I was at Doc's office on Park Avenue, I told him the little finger on my right hand has been bothering me for 2 ½ weeks.

"Why not X-ray it and see if there's anything wrong?" I said.

"Why not?" Doc said.

When he returned with the X-rays, he was shaking his head.

"Broken?" I asked.

"Yes, Vic."

The break was near the first knuckle.

"There's nothing much we can do about it now," Doc said. "It's starting to mend by itself. You can play but it's going to take twice the time to mend properly because it wasn't in a cast."

"The hell with it," I said. "I'm going to play Sunday no matter what. I'll just be a little more careful with the thumb and finger."

FEBRUARY 23

It felt good to practice today without that damn cast on my hand. The thumb is still a little tender and so is the finger, but I'm ready to play. I told the Cat that when he phoned from Oakland, where the club plays tonight.

I was napping on the couch when he phoned. He said he had already checked with the doctor and was happy to learn I'll be ready by Sunday. Cat told me he sent Rod Gilbert back to New York. Rod came down with the flu after competing in those mini-Olympics in Florida early this week. Pro athletes from various sports were invited to compete in the two-day event. Rod represented hockey and fared well, especially in tennis and golf. He had to leave his hockey stick at home.

FEBRUARY 24

The Golden Seals sealed us. They won last night's game, 5–3. What a time for us to stumble. If we had won we could have pulled to within four points of Montreal and opened a four-point lead over Boston.

Now I know I can't waste any more time sitting on my duff. I practiced this morning with my son, Jeffrey. Bruce MacGregor showed up, too, with his son, Bradley. We had a father-and-son scrimmage to test my hand. No problems, thank God.

FEBRUARY 25

We played a wild and wooly game with the North Stars tonight. This one had everything. We wiped out a 4–1 Minnesota lead to win, 6–4. Ratelle scored the winning goal on a power play with two minutes remaining.

That battling Italian, Ed Giacomin, got into a fight with Bill Goldsworthy late in the game. Then Cesare Maniago left the Minnesota net and skated to midice to get into the rumble. What a sight that was.

It started when Giacomin and Goldsworthy collided near the net. When Goldy got up, he took a swipe at

Eddie. "He whacked me across the wrist," Eddie said. "I don't mind getting checked when I leave the net, but Goldy really whacked me. That's when I tried to retaliate."

Giacomin took off after Goldy, chasing him all the way to center ice. When Dale Rolfe put a headlock on Goldy and threw him to the ice, Maniago made his move. He is very tall and looked like a camel in skates as he moved up ice, half running and half skating in his bulky pads.

By now everybody was paired off. I grabbed Doug Mohns, the North Stars' veteran defenseman who wears a hairpiece off the ice. Somebody asked me later why I grabbed Mohns. "He was the oldest guy on the ice," I said. The truth is I had to be careful I didn't injure my hands again. This was my first game in two weeks. I got a goal in the second period, and it helped give me a little boost.

I had some fun with the Cat when Giacomin was penalized for his fracas with Goldsworthy. Emile waved and called me to the bench.

"You serve Eddie's penalty," he said.

"But the ref won't let me," I said.

I was fibbing, of course. I was hoping he would get somebody else to serve the penalty. There were only a couple of minutes left in the game, and I wanted to take another turn on the ice.

The Cat wasn't about to buy that.

"Get into that penalty box," he shouted.

"But I told you the ref won't let me," I repeated.

"Like hell he won't. Get your ass over there."

"A fine way to treat your captain," I said.

That really broke up the guys. They laughed and started heckling me. I laughed, too, as I skated to the box.

FEBRUARY 27

The boss frequently gives us Mondays off to catch our collective breaths, but he had us on the ice yesterday,

91

working our butts off. "No more days off from now on," the Cat said. "We've got to start thinking about the play-offs."

Following practice, Emile and I attended a hockey press luncheon. The Islanders were represented by Earl Ingarfield and Spinner Spencer. Most players don't like to sound off at these luncheons, mainly because the coach is there. But this didn't hamper Spencer. He said he wasn't surprised that the Islanders were in last place. "We're not aggressive enough," Spinner said. He then offered a few other frank observations on the poor Islanders.

When he finished his little speech, Spencer turned to Ingarfield and whispered, "Did I say anything wrong, Earl? I still need a ride back to Long Island." Ingarfield grinned, weakly.

We were guests last night at a reception staged by Mayor John Lindsay and his wife, Mary, at Gracie Mansion. All the players attended, along with their wives and children. The mayor presented keys to the city to the Cat, Bill Jennings, and Irving Mitchell Felt, the Garden boss.

As the team captain it was my duty to speak for the players. I thanked the mayor and then said, "Have fun, the drinks are on me." I later was presented with a bill for sixteen hundred dollars. "That covers the cost of the drinks," Bob Malito said. He is an aide to the mayor. It was a fake bill, but I went along with the gag. "I'll pay it off on the installment plan . . . fifty cents a week," I said.

We play the Black Hawks tomorrow night at the Garden. They have a new center: Ralph Backstom. He was picked up from the Los Angeles Kings in a trade for Dan Maloney. The Hawks needed an experienced center because Stan Mikita is out with a broken foot. They got a good one in Backstom, but they had to surrender a tremendous kid. Maloney is young and aggressive, likes to hit, and doesn't back away from anybody.

92

Don't talk to me about luck. Mine has been all bad lately. I got hit in the face with a puck while we were playing a 3–3 tie against the Black Hawks last night.

It happened in the second period. We had a power play on and the puck went back to Walt Tkaczuk on the left point. I skated to the net just as Walt shot. The puck deflected off somebody's stick and struck me on the left cheekbone, close to the nose. I went down and the guys gathered around me. When I got up, Frank Paice looked at me and said, "Wow, you're going to need some stitches." Trainers are so perceptive.

I took five stitches, came back for the third period, and finished the game. By then the left side of my face was swollen and I looked like I had been run over by a twelve-wheel truck.

The doc gave me some pain-killing pills, but I didn't sleep too well last night. When I got up this morning, I looked in the mirror and didn't recognize myself. The cheek was swollen, my eyes were blackened, and I had a helluva headache.

I went back to bed and stayed there until about 4:00 P.M. when I drove my boy, Jeffrey, and Bradley Mac-Gregor to a rink for their hockey game. As soon as their game was over, I drove home and went back to bed.

The swelling in my cheek is starting to subside, so I practiced with the team today. We then caught a late-afternoon plane for Detroit. We play the Red Wings at the Olympia tomorrow night.

Ab DeMarco wasn't with us on the flight to Detroit.

He has been traded to St. Louis for Mike Murphy, a right winger who grew up in the Ranger farm system. I'll miss Abbie. He's a good kid with a lot of class. While he was with us, the poor guy was slowed down by an injury jinx.

Look who's talking.

We also got Sheldon Kannegiesser from Pittsburgh for "future considerations." How are they going to fit that guy's name on the back of his home jersey? Sheldon also is a product of the Ranger organization. He's a defenseman who was farmed out by the Penguins this season when he ran into trouble with his coach, Red Kelly. Now Kelly's gone and Sheldon is with the Rangers. The wheels keep turning.

MARCH 4

Remember that TV commercial for aspirin that showed little mallets pounding on a man's brain? That's the way my head feels today. It has felt that way since I got hit with the puck last Wednesday. I've had persistent headaches and my vision is blurred.

I took regular line shifts against the Red Wings last night. We won the game, 6–3, and I had two goals and two assists. Ratelle had a goal and three assists, while Gilbert picked up a goal and two assists. That gave our line eleven points—our best output of the season.

Don't ask me how I managed to play against the Wings. It's a funny thing, you know. Sometime when you're feeling your worst, you play your best. I was having trouble seeing the puck, but I still got those two goals.

We flew back to New York right after the game because we play the Vancouver Canucks at the Garden tonight. The Canucks are having a lot of internal problems; the players are fighting among themselves and with their coach,

Vic Stasiuk. They were wiped out by the Islanders, 9–3, last night so they shouldn't give us any trouble.

MARCH 5

The Canucks beat us, 4–3, proving you can't take any team lightly. We had a number of opportunities early in the game, but couldn't click. We were passing when we should have been shooting and vice versa.

Our dressing room was very quiet after the game. We blew two points at a bad time. We're into the final month of the season and we know we can't afford to lose to a team like Vancouver.

We picked up another defenseman just before the trading deadline last night. He's Bert Marshall, who had been serving as captain of the California Golden Seals. Emile got him for "future considerations." I'm sure Bert will give us a big lift, but he can't become captain of the Rangers. Only one captain to a team, Bert.

I had to skip practice today because of my damn headaches. If they don't clear up by tomorrow I'm going to visit a specialist.

MARCH 6

Have you ever had eighteen needles stuck into your head? I have, and it's a weird experience.

I visited a neurologist after practice today. His name is Dr. Jerome Block, and his office is on Park Avenue in Manhattan. He gave me an encephalogram test to check if pressure on the brain was causing my headaches. It's the same type of test they give boxers after they suffer a knockout or catch too many punches on the head.

The equipment that the doctor used for the test was too elaborate for me to explain. But the needles. Wow! They were about a half inch long, and they were pushed just deep enough into my scalp so that the machine could take a reading of my brain.

As I lay there hooked up by wires and electrodes to the brain-wave machine, I felt I was ready to send out an S-O-S. I don't know if I was shaking or not; I tried to act brave, but I was scared as hell.

Dr. Block said he would turn over the results of the test to Emile before our game against the Philadelphia Flyers tomorrow night. Meanwhile, I'll keep my fingers crossed.

MARCH 7

The tests turned out negative. Dr. Block telephoned this afternoon and said there was no evidence of pressure on the brain and that nothing appeared to be scrambled up there. Just a concussion. I was relieved to get that news, but I'm still feeling rotten.

The doctor explained that different people suffer different reactions to concussions. He suggested lots of rest—and no more hockey for a while.

I had traveled into Manhattan for tonight's game against the Flyers, but headed home before the players took the ice. I climbed into bed and listened to the game on the radio. Bill Flett, the guy with the beard, scored in the third period to earn Philly a 2–2 tie. It was Flett's thirty-seventh goal of the season. He claims he has the strength of Samson since growing that beard. Don't knock it.

Slats Sather got into a fight with Dave Schultz in the first period. Schultz got in the first punch, a pretty good right hand, and most of the reporters gave him the decision. But what the hell, Slats was giving away about three inches and twenty-five pounds. If I know Slats, he'll get his revenge on Schultz some other time.

I've done nothing but sleep for the past two days. It's a wonder I don't have bed sores. I finally left the house today and wandered down the street to buy a newspaper. I guess I startled some of the neighbors because I had a three-day beard and looked like a hermit.

During most of the time that I lay around the house I felt like I had been drugged. My vision was blurred, so I had trouble reading, and I gave up trying to watch television.

I felt better today, though, and was able to watch the telecast of the Rangers' game in Pittsburgh. The guys jumped off to a 4–1 lead, then had to work like hell to preserve a 5–4 victory. Porky Park got the winning goal.

MARCH 11

There's nothing like a goal to make a man forget his troubles—and his headaches.

We played Toronto in one of those nationally televised Sunday afternoon games today. I drove into the city and had a meeting with Emile in his office prior to the game.

"How do you feel, Vic?" he asked.

"Not bad," I said. "You know how I like to play against Toronto. I'd like to dress and maybe play a little bit."

That's exactly what I did. Emile kept me on the bench until late in the first period, when I climbed over the boards and joined Ratelle and Gilbert on the ice. About twelve seconds later, Leafs' defenseman Dave Fortier made a bad clearing pass in the Toronto end and the puck wound up on my stick.

"Look what I've got here," I mumbled to myself.

I took a couple of strides into the left face-off circle and really ripped it. The puck landed just inside the far corner of the net.

The headaches were gone now. I skated back to the bench and Pete Stemkowski was chuckling. "That's your goal for the day," he said. "You may as well take the rest of the day off." Teddy Irvine sat there shaking his head. He said, "Damn, I play game after game and work like hell for my goals. You come back and need only twelve seconds to get a goal. Lucky stiff."

I was lucky—and happy, too. The goal gave me a great feeling. It gave us a 2–0 lead and we wound up winning the game, 4–2. I wonder how the folks back in Toronto liked that one.

MARCH 12

A big day for Bruce MacGregor. He had the cast removed from his ankle last Friday and skated for the first time at practice today. It was an optional workout. Bert Marshall showed up, along with Steve Vickers, Gilles Villemure, and Peter McDuffe. I skated, too, and felt okay.

MARCH 14

Chicago was almost springlike today. The temperature was in the sixties and there was no breeze blowing in off Lake Michigan. We flew in here last night for a game against the Black Hawks tonight.

I spent part of the afternoon walking around the Loop. City Hall isn't too far from our hotel, and as I walked by the building I thought of Mayor Daley and some of the decisions he would be making during the day. I don't envy any man who has to make decisions—minor or major.

Now I'm back in my room, resting before the game. Daydreaming would be a better word for it. This has been a strange season for me thus far. I've missed a few games, returned for two or three, and then rested again. It's a hard feeling to explain, other than to say it's strange.

I'm sure a lot of hockey players go through this and feel the same way. You can't afford to miss too many games; you feel you're letting the team down. But you don't want to play unless you're sure you can contribute something.

The Black Hawks beat us, 4–2. I played and drew an assist on a second-period goal by Rod Gilbert. Gene Carr had a scuffle with Keith Magnuson and came out of it with a fat lip. Gene got the worse part of it, but he hung in there and showed he wasn't going to back down. I gave him points for that because Magnuson is much bigger than Gene.

I liked Magnuson's comment after the fight. He said, "That's one of the few fights I ever won." An honest man. Maggie is also a very intense person. In order to be effective he has to be aggressive. He'll challenge you, but I can't ever remember him taking a cheap shot. He takes a lot of punishment and comes back for more. He also knows how to dish it out.

After the game I had supper with Bobby Rousseau and Ron Harris and Jean Ratelle. We discussed the few games we have left in the regular season and how we'll have to correct things. We're giving the other teams a lot of breakaways. Maybe we've become too offensive-minded and should start concentrating on defensive hockey.

Emile always points out at our team meetings that it's not what you make but what you leave. This is applied mainly to billiards, but it also has a bearing on other sports, including hockey.

MARCH 15

We're back in Toronto for the first time since early in the season. We arrived here from Chicago at about 2:00

P.M. and went right to Maple Leaf Gardens for practice. We skated for forty-five minutes without touching a puck. Emile felt we needed the skate and nobody bitched—not to him, anyway.

As we were finishing our free skating, Stemkowski said, "How about one more trip around the ice, Emile?" Peter was only kidding, of course, but the Cat made him do it, all by himself. Then Bruce MacGregor joined him. After skating so long, the ice got quite rough, and Bruce hit a rut in the ice and twisted his ankle. MacGregor came back to the dressing room rubbing his ankle; then it started to swell. That should set him back a few more days.

After practice, we finally got around to initiating Steve Vickers into the club by working him over with the scissors. This is an old team ritual for rookies. We got some white tape and taped Vickers to a table. Brad Park got the scissors and started cutting off hair. He concentrated on one eyebrow and one sideburn, so Steve looked a little lopsided when Brad was finished.

The worst thing you can do under these circumstances is to fight back. Gene Carr fought like hell last year and almost lost an ear. Vickers was smarter. He remained calm throughout the "operation."

MARCH 16

We practiced again today at Maple Leaf Gardens. Andy Bathgate was there along with a mutual friend, Ike Oka. Andy and I later drove to Burlington, Ontario, so I could get a look at our new Indian Wells golf course. It was something to see. A lot of work has gone into the course since I last saw it.

I wasn't feeling too well when I got back to Toronto. More headaches, more dizziness. I had dinner and went to my room at eight-thirty. I tried to watch a televised game between the Red Wings and Bruins in Detroit, but my eyes were bothering me. I shut off the set with the score tied in the second period.

After snoozing for a while, I turned the set back on. It was the third period and the score was still tied. With eighteen seconds left to play, Doug Roberts scored from the blue line for Boston. He caught Denis DeJordy out of his net and out of the picture.

Damn that DeJordy. He let the Bruins pick up two important points on us. Why in hell didn't he stay in the net where he belongs?

MARCH 17

St. Patrick's Day in Toronto. There're a lot of Irishmen in this city, and they did a lot of celebrating tonight. So did a lot of other people after the Maple Leafs beat us, 7–5. We didn't just get beat—we got embarrassed. We blew a 4–1 lead by letting the Leafs pull even in the second period. They put the game out of reach by scoring three more times before the midpoint of the final period.

Sitting on the bench, I couldn't help thinking of all my friends in the stands watching this massacre. We're so much stronger than the Leafs. We were picked to finish first and win the Stanley Cup. How in hell could we play as bad as we did tonight?

It was hard to face my friends and relatives from the Toronto area after the game. I did it, but I didn't like it. I was happy over the fact that the Toronto fans didn't boo me during the game. They seem to be on my side now.

We're now two points back of second-place Boston with a game in hand. I figure we can still finish second and get that extra home game for the play-offs. But not if we continue to blow leads the way we did tonight.

Toronto was hit by one of those late-winter rain-, sleet-, and snowstorms last night, and we were lucky our flight wasn't canceled. We arrived back in New York at 3:00 A.M., got up at noon, and had a team meeting at 1:00 P.M.

Emile had a few things to say—nothing complimentary—and then held a sort of open forum. He suggested we all speak up. "If you've got any ideas, let's hear 'em," he said.

Giacomin was the first to speak. He said, "We've been too loose out there. We're taking everything for granted. We've got to tighten up and be more defensive-minded."

Tkaczuk was next. His voice is a little high-pitched and doesn't seem to fit his husky body. Somebody yelled "Speak up, Walter," and he did. "Jeez, we're not checking. We're not getting two men in fast enough to fight for the puck. We're hesitating when we should be jumping in there. Let's smarten up."

For Walter, that was a big speech.

And so it went, with each guy getting up and speaking his mind.

Sather, no shrinking violet, made several good points. Slats said, "We got that big lead at Toronto and then we backed off. We let up. That's not our style. Once we abandon our game plan, we get careless and start to struggle and the other team sees this and we're in trouble. We've got to stick to our game plan and show no mercy."

It was now my turn. I said I agreed with most of the suggestions offered and made a pitch for self-discipline. "We've got to have pride in who we are and what we're doing," I said. "I'm talking about our conduct off the ice. Nobody wants to stay up and make bed checks, and that shouldn't be necessary anyway. So let's pull together and watch ourselves.

"We're pros and we should know our limit. If a man is a two-beer man, that's when he should stop. Another guy can handle four beers. Okay, that's his limit. That's when he should stop and hit the sack and get a good night's sleep. We have only ourselves to blame if we don't stick by our training rules."

After the meeting we went back to the Penn Plaza Hotel for our pregame meal. I felt okay during the afternoon, but in the dressing room I leaned over to put on my skates, straightened up, and became dizzy. The room was spinning around, so I sat down for a few minutes and then went out on the ice for our warmup. I still felt a little woozy and went back to the dressing room and took off my skates. When I tried to walk across the room, I almost fell on my face.

Dr. John Grozine, one of our team physicians, was there. I was now as white as a ghost. The doctor got one look at me and went to Emile and told him he was sending me home.

I drove home with Myrna sitting alongside of me. I could sense Myrna was worried about my condition. She has seen me play with broken fingers and hands, but this was something different. This was head trouble. She was concerned about that—and so was I.

MARCH 19

I wasn't feeling much better when I got up this morning. I went to bed soon after I got home last night and listened to our game against the St. Louis Blues. Mike Murphy got two goals and Gilles Villemure was great in goal and we won, 3–1.

Murphy had gone scoreless in fifteen straight games, so I was happy for him. He was pretty happy, too, because only a month ago he was playing for the Blues and now he had broken out of his slump against his old teammates.

I paid a return visit to Dr. Block, the neurologist, this afternoon. He took more tests and arrived at the same conclusion: I was still feeling the affects of the concussion and it was just a matter of time before I shook it. No medication, though. All he prescribed was rest, lots of rest.

The guys took off today on their last road trip of the regular season. They play at Minnesota tomorrow night, at Atlanta Thursday night, and at Boston Saturday afternoon. Maybe I can join them in Boston Saturday. Maybe.

MARCH 21

Rod Seiling suffered a broken collarbone last night at Minnesota. We beat the North Stars, 6–1, but that's secondary now. I watched the game on TV and winced when Rod got hit by Fred Barrett. Rod had just taken a shot and was blind-sided by Barrett. It looked like a clean check; Rod just didn't see Barrett coming.

As I watched the TV replay and saw Rod skating to the bench, holding his left shoulder, I figured, well, it's either a separated shoulder or a broken collarbone. It was the collarbone.

Now I'm sitting here at home and thinking of all the things that have gone wrong with our club this season. We've all worked so hard and it's so disheartening to have it all break down with all these injuries. I'm also thinking of Emile Francis. He's worked harder than any of us. He's the guy I really feel sorry for.

Rod Seiling must be feeling pretty rotten, too. He was looking forward to the play-offs, but his season is over.

People frequently ask me about Rod, what he means to the club. You look at the defensemen in the league, and there are guys who score more points than Rod. His value, though, isn't in the points he scores. He helps you in different ways—his experience and his ability to control the puck. He rarely gives the puck away, makes a bad pass or a bad play.

Off the ice, Rod likes to be by himself a lot. I don't mean to hint he ducks the other guys; it's just that he has other interests. He's very serious-minded. On the team bus, he'll sit alone after a game and nobody bothers him. If he wants to brood, we let him brood. If he wants to join in the fun, he's always welcome. He's the team player representative and a good one because he has a keen mind. He's also one helluvan underrated defenseman.

MARCH 22

The doctor said it would be okay for me to skate today, so I drove to Skateland in the morning and gave it a try. I had to quit after fifteen minutes because I felt so weak. Maybe it's because I've been spending so much time resting.

I came home and slept all afternoon, then took my son, Jeffrey, to one of his hockey games. He's on the same team with Brad MacGregor and Richard Rousseau. They're in the finals of a tournament for squirts.

It's exciting for me to watch Jeff play hockey. He really takes the game seriously. I've always told him that I'm not too interested in whether he wins or loses, just that he does his best. Naturally, I'd like to see his team win for his sake, but I feel there is too much pressure placed on these boys. Jeff is only eight, and the main thing for him and kids of his age is to let them enjoy playing.

Sitting in the stands and listening to the parents yell at their kids and urging them on . . . well, it makes me wonder. They're creating added pressure for the boys, and this is bad. The kids didn't play too well today, though they did win. Richard Rousseau scored the winning goal.

I tuned in on the team's game at Atlanta tonight. We won, 4-1. It's really hard for me to sit still and listen to these games on the radio. I've been so active for so many years, and now I find myself confined to the house like an invalid. It's also turned me into a grouch. Life around the house hasn't been too pleasant lately. Myrna and the kids have had to put up with a lot of guff from me.

MARCH 23

I skated again today for about thirty minutes. I felt a little better, so I brought my skates home in case I decided to fly to Boston. We play the Bruins there tomorrow afternoon.

The headaches started to bother me again after lunch. I was napping when Emile called from Boston.

"How are you feeling?" he asked.

"Not too good," I said. "I don't think I'd better try to fly up there."

"Okay, Vic, don't rush it. Lay low for a couple of more days and we'll see how you feel after the weekend."

I hung up the receiver and cursed to myself. This thing is eating at me. Maybe if I went to Boston and rested until game time I'd be okay. But what's the use? If I'm not feeling well, Emile is better off using somebody else in my place—somebody who is healthy.

MARCH 24

Another dismal day in front of the TV set. I watched our afternoon game against the Bruins, and it spoiled my dinner. Jacques Plante threw a 3-0 shutout at our guys. Bobby Orr set up Greg Sheppard on a breakaway early in the first period. Sheppard beat Gilles Villemure with a great move, and as it turned out that was all the margin Plante needed.

I must tell you a Bobby Orr story now. My daughter, Julie, is one of his fans. She wrote him a letter and asked for his autograph. She received a nice reply and an autographed picture from Bobby. He is one of the class guys in the NHL.

If you're wondering how a daughter of the Ranger team captain could develop a fondness for any member of the Bruins, let me offer this explanation for Julie: She is a Bobby Orr fan, not a Bruins' fan. This doesn't prevent her from rooting just as hard as the rest of the family for her dad and the Rangers.

And speaking of the Hadfield family, Jeffrey's team won the tournament championship this morning. He scored the winning goal in the second overtime period and was smiling from ear to ear when he got home. Good for Jeff. Now if his dad could only wind up on a championship team one of these days.

MARCH 25

I picked up Bruce MacGregor this morning and we drove to Skateland with our sons and skated for a half hour. Bruce is looking for all the ice time he can get now that the play-offs are approaching. His ankle seems to be getting stronger with each passing day. I wish I could say the same for my condition.

It tears at my insides when I walk into our dressing room and see the others getting dressed and know I'm not going to play. I experienced that sensation again before our game against the Minnesota North Stars tonight. Then I went up into the television booth at Madison Square Garden and watched the North Stars win, 2–1.

Bill Chadwick and Sal Marchiano, the TV announcers,

used me as a guest analyst. It all looks so easy when you watch the plays develop from such a high perch. You see the good plays and some of the mistakes the guys are making—how they pass when they should shoot and vice versa.

I can understand now how the fans get on the players at times, because it looks so easy from the stands. But put those same fans on the ice and they'd soon learn how different it is. Hindsight is a great thing. It permits you to second-guess a play or a player. The fans, though, should remember this: A player is permitted only one guess. And most times a play develops so fast in hockey you can't even guess; you have to act quickly.

Bob Nevin didn't play for the North Stars tonight. I guess he's in coach Jackie Gordon's doghouse. That's a shame, because Nevvy has all kinds of experience and could help any club getting ready for the play-offs.

MARCH 26

I'm back in harness again, and what a great feeling. I put on my equipment for a regular practice this morning for the first time in nine days. We play the Bruins at home Wednesday night and I want to be ready for that one. It's our last regular-season meeting with Boston and figures to be a play-off preview.

I felt so chipper after practice that I drove into Manhattan and attended a cocktail party given by Eastman Chemical, a subsidiary of Eastman Kodak. I make personal appearances for them when time allows. They have other sports personalities involved in this work—guys like Willie Mays and Fran Tarkenton, Earl Morrall and Billy Talbert. I like mingling with them, shooting the breeze and exchanging stories.

Bruce Roberts, one of the company's vice presidents,

introduced me to the guests. After shaking hands with a few people and signing autographs, I drove back to Long Island and was in bed by 10:00 P.M.

MARCH 27

You can tell it's getting close to the play-offs—Glen Sather is getting bitchy and yelling at everybody. He was really wound up at practice today. I like to kid around with him, so after practice I said, "Why don't you knock off the complaining, Slats." He looked at me and snarled, "Up yours, captain." Tsk, tsk.

MARCH 28

I heard something tonight that really shocked me. While we were losing to the Bruins, 6–3, the Garden fans started singing, "Goodbye, Emile, we hate to see you go." Now, isn't that a helluva note. Why blame the coach because we couldn't stop Phil Esposito?

Phil was something else tonight. He scored four goals—all four under different situations. He had a power-play goal, a short-handed goal, one that he banked in from behind the net, and the final one was scored in an empty net.

When the game was over, somebody asked Phil if he heard the fans serenading Emile. "Yeah, I heard them," he said. "But they can't get rid of the Cat . . . he's too smart." Ain't that the truth.

Emile has done another great coaching job this season. He's guided us into the play-offs for the seventh straight year. No other coach in the NHL can match that. I suppose the fans were upset tonight because the Bruins clinched second place. We're pretty upset, too, but why blame the Cat?

Now for a personal word or two about Phil Esposito.

109

He's enjoyed another great season, no doubt about it. He's a great opportunist who positions himself in front of the net or midway in the slot, and he scores a lot of goals on tip-ins or rebounds. I'm not knocking him for that; I've gotten my share of goals that way. But I don't think his wingers get enough credit.

Ken Hodge and Wayne Cashman work hard for Phil. They're like foot soldiers. They barge into the corners, fight for the puck, and when they get it they set up Phil in front. Phil gets the goals and the credit, but don't overlook the work of Hodge and Cashman.

I got into my first game in almost two weeks against the Bruins. I was a little weak at the start, but felt better as the game went along. With a couple of more practices and games under my belt I figure I'll be close to 100 percent again.

P.S.: I almost forgot about an incident that happened earlier today when we posed for our annual team picture. Bill Jennings, the club president, and Irving Mitchell Felt, chairman of the board, arrived late. Somebody reminded them that when the players show up late they are fined a hundred dollars, so we expected them to add two hundred dollars to the players' kitty.

Mr. Jennings laughed and said, "Okay, we'll make it up to you guys when we give you the checks for winning the Cup."

Fair enough.

MARCH 30

One of the best bodychecks of the year was thrown by Rod Gilbert at practice today. The victim was Glen Sather. Rod really laid it on him. Whenever Slats gets mad, his face turns as red as a beet. Some of the guys call him "Tomato." Well, he was really a tomato face when he picked himself off the ice and started chasing Rod around the rink.

I yelled, "Go get him, Tomato. Don't let Rod get away with that."

By the time Sather caught Rod he had calmed down. But Glen still had to get in the last word. He said, "You'd better keep your head up from now on, Rod, or I'll get you for that." Everybody laughed, including Rod. The old Tomato was only kidding.

We flew to Montreal later in the day for our game against the Canadiens tomorrow afternoon. After checking into the Château Champlain, some of us examined Rod Gilbert's newest business venture. He's a partner in a discothèque in the downtown section of Montreal. We had a few beers there and got back to the hotel early.

Our game against the Canadiens could be a play-off preview, so we want to be ready for them. We know what we have to do against them: play a close-checking game and execute.

MARCH 31

The Canadiens beat us, 5–1. We forgot to check and we didn't execute.

The game was only ninety-three seconds old when Jimmy Neilson got caught holding the puck in the crease. Jacques Lemaire was awarded a penalty shot and beat Eddie Giacomin with a pretty good shot. Giacomin had been out since March 17 with a strained right knee, and where do you suppose Lemaire aimed his shot? Right at Eddie's right knee. Eddie tried to kick at it but missed, and the Canadiens were off and running.

We wind up our regular season against Detroit tomorrow night at Madison Square Garden. It's a big game for the Red Wings. They've carried their fight with Buffalo for the fourth and final play-off spot down to the wire.

The Red Wings didn't make it. They ended their season by holding us to a 3–3 tie. It wasn't good enough, because Buffalo beat St. Louis, 3–1. That enabled the Sabres to finish fourth. You have to give the Sabres credit; they made the play-offs in their third year in the league.

In our game against the Red Wings, Billy Fairbairn and Jean Ratelle scored in the first period. I got the third goal in the final period on a beautiful pass from Ratty.

During the intermission between the second and third periods I was in the corridor outside our dressing room working on one of my sticks when Bruce Norris walked up to me. He's the owner of the Red Wings, a big, strong guy who likes to arm wrestle.

"Okay, Vic," he said, "let's fight it out to see who wins this game. Just you and me . . . winner take all."

"No thanks, you're too damn big for me, Bruce," I said.

We both laughed then, but deep down I knew we were really hurting Bruce Norris and his team. It was not a time for joking.

Bruce is different from most of the club owners I know. He takes an active interest in the club, attends a lot of the Wings' road games, and seems to enjoy mixing with the players, even guys like me from the enemy camp.

So the lines are drawn now for the play-offs. We open our series against the Bruins at Boston Wednesday night. The other openers that night will be Buffalo at Montreal, Philadelphia at Minnesota, and St. Louis at Chicago.

We're in Fitchburg, Massachusetts, preparing for the Bruins. We checked in here last night. We caught a flight to

Boston after our game against Detroit, then traveled by bus to Fitchburg. I fell asleep on the bus, and when we got here I looked around and said, "My God, we're way out in the sticks."

"What's a Fitchburg?" Rod Gilbert asked.

"I don't know," Pete Stemkowski said, "but everybody claims it's a one-horse town except the local streetcleaner."

Actually, it's a pretty nice little town located in central Massachusetts and about a one-hour drive from Boston. There is a new sports complex here with two regulation-size hockey rinks, which is one of the reasons Emile brought us here. Another reason is that it's so quiet you can almost hear the grass grow.

Emile didn't advise the press where we were headed when we left New York. He wanted us to get away from the hustle and bustle of play-off pressure, relax and think about nothing but hockey. He found the right place.

In preparing for the play-offs, it's not so much a physical thing because we've just gone through a seventy-eight-game schedule. We're in pretty good shape physically; now we have to prepare ourselves mentally for the Bruins.

After today's practice, we had lunch and then looked at movies of our last two regular-season games against the Bruins. They were more like horror movies because we lost both games, but we did notice some Boston weaknesses that we hope to exploit.

Gilles Villemure heard there was a bowling alley in town and couldn't wait to check it out. We went around making bets that he could average 160 for 3 games. He must have covered about $100 in bets, then headed for the bowling alley with some of the fellows. Gilly got quite a surprise. They bowl duckpins around here, and Gilly is strictly a 10-pin man. But he didn't back down. He rolled a 90 in his first game and that hurt him. It also cost him $100.

Our Fitchburg hideaway isn't a hideaway any longer. At practice today I noticed Tim Moriarty of *Newsday* peering at us through the large glass entrance door to the rink. He is my collaborator on this book, but I never told him we would be hiding out in Fitchburg. Tim just stumbled onto us. He was visiting his parents in Southbridge, Massachusetts, and somebody tipped him we were holed up here.

He showed up at the rink with a nephew, Steve Jones, who is sports editor of the Southbridge *News*. They were joined later by Leigh Montville of the Boston *Globe* and some local writers.

I guess Emile was surprised to see Tim and the other writers. But once the cat was out of the bag, Emile joined them at lunch and held an informal press conference.

We looked at more films after today's practice and now I'm lying down in my room at the Thunderbird Motor Lodge and thinking about the season and the play-offs and the Bruins. It's been a strange season for myself and the team. We were hit hard by injuries, but we stayed close to the pack until the final two or three weeks, when Montreal pulled ahead of us and then Boston beat us out of second place.

As for myself, it was one injury after another. But I had to keep going; I had a lot to prove—that the fifty goals I scored last season wasn't a fluke. I was reasonably satisfied with my play—when I got to play. I got into sixty-three games and totaled twenty-eight goals and sixty-two points. Now that's a long way from fifty goals, but it still represented the second-best output for me in my twelve years with the Rangers.

Now we're heading into the play-offs, and it's like another season—a time to make up for any past disappointments. I've been feeling pretty good the past few days—

no headaches, thank God. The Bruins are good, but I'm sure we'll beat them. I'm just as certain that the team that wins our series will go on and win the Cup.

What did I tell you? We beat the Bruins in the series opener, 6–2. Okay, so it's only one game, but it's very important, especially when you win it in the other fellows' building.

We went into the game with what Pete Stemkowski calls "quiet confidence." I could feel it on the bus ride from Fitchburg to Boston this morning. We said goodbye to Fitchburg at eleven o'clock. It was a very quiet bus ride; everybody seemed to be concentrating on what we had to do to beat the Bruins. The trip took about ninety minutes, and we checked into the Sonesta in Cambridge during the noon hour.

We had our pregame steak, napped for a while, and then headed for Boston Garden. The guys were still quiet in the locker room as we dressed for the game. No horsing around now. Strictly business.

The game started at a slow pace. Our game plan was to keep the puck away from Esposito and Orr . . . by sending two men in early and harassing them with solid fore-checking. It worked. Espo didn't have a shot on net until the third period. His linemates, Hodge and Cashman, didn't get off a single shot. Orr had three shots but no goals.

Our line was matched against Espo's line most of the night. We didn't score either, but we accomplished what we set out to do: to bottle up Phil.

Tkaczuk and Park had two goals apiece for us. MacGregor and Stemkowski had the others against Jacques Plante, who looked pretty shaky most of the night.

The pattern of the game was established early. Giacomin went behind the net to stop the puck from whipping around the backboards and Hodge hit him. Park jumped in, then Ted Irvine came out of nowhere and grabbed Hodge. Ted and Ken squared off and had a pretty good fight.

That really gave us a big lift. Once the fellows realized we were going to stick together and not take any of Boston's bullying tactics, we all played better. It's one of the things you have to do against a team like the Bruins. Show them who's boss right away.

Irvine also had a fight with Orr. They had been shoving each other around early, and in the second period they got their sticks up, then dropped their gloves and went at it. I watched the Bruins bench while Teddy and Bobby were battling, and most of their guys looked bewildered. I think they realized then that we weren't going to take any crap from them.

Irvine actually suckered Orr into the fight, and each drew seven minutes in penalties. It turned out to be a good trade for us. Teddy is an honest, hard worker, but Orr is far more important to his team. We scored three goals while Bobby was cooling off in the penalty box.

Esposito was really teed off after the game. When a reporter approached him in the Bruins' dressing room, Phil snapped, "Don't bother me . . . I'm not talking."

The reporter snapped back, "I remember you when you were a nice guy, Phil."

"Oh, yeah," Phil answered. "Well, I'm not a bleeping nice guy any more, so get lost."

I guess Phil was a little frustrated because he normally is very cooperative with reporters. Our job now is to keep him frustrated for the rest of the series.

APRIL 5

The city of Boston is about to sink into Massachusetts Bay. We beat the Bruins again, 4–2. The defending champs are

116

really reeling now. They've lost the first two games on their home ice and they've also lost Phil Esposito.

Phil was carrying the puck down the right side in the second period of tonight's game when Ronnie Harris cut him down with a solid but clean bodycheck. Phil grabbed his right knee as soon as he hit the ice. He was obviously in great pain.

Hodge and Cashman helped their buddy to his feet and led him to the dressing room. Phil later was taken to Massachusetts General Hospital and got the bad news. X-rays disclosed he tore a lateral ligament in his right knee. He faces possible surgery.

The Bruins are going to find it pretty tough to bounce back without big No. 7 in the lineup. Phil means so much to that club. He kills penalties, is the triggerman on the power play, and takes his regular shift.

Derek Sanderson used a mod phrase in describing Espo's loss. He said, "That's all she wrote," which could be translated into goodbye lover, goodbye Bruins.

Bep Guidolin, the Bruins' coach, said it another way: "The coffin isn't closed yet, but they've got the hammer and nails ready."

We didn't come through the second game unscathed. Hodge fell on Giacomin during a second-period pileup in front of the crease. Eddie came out of it with a pinched nerve in his neck and had to take the rest of the night off. Villemure took over and preserved the victory like a good relief pitcher.

None of the Bruins rapped Harris for putting Espo in the hospital. They know Ronnie is tough but clean. He just happened to hit Phil as he was falling to the ice, and Phil's right knee was extended and vulnerable. Ronnie has eleven "hits" in that second game, which is really something. A "hit," incidentally, doesn't mean putting a guy into the stands with a bodycheck. You get credit for a "hit" just by taking a man out of the play. And Ronnie spent most of the night doing that.

We flew out of Boston on an Allegheny Airlines charter and landed at Westchester County Airport in White Plains. A bus took us from there to the Westchester Country Club, which will be our "home" for the next two games at Madison Square Garden.

We were greeted at the airport by two men carrying a huge Ranger banner. One was our bus driver; the other man was John Maguire, the general manager of the Westchester Country Club. Bill Jennings also was there, along with his wife, Betsy, and daughter, Lisa.

After checking into our rooms, we gathered downstairs for a little postmidnight snack of sandwiches and beer. I had a couple of beers and hit the sack at about 1:30 A.M.

APRIL 6

Phil Esposito was interviewed by Tim Moriarty today in the hospital, and Phil absolved Ronnie Harris of any blame. Espo said, "Tell Ronnie there's no hard feelings. It wasn't his fault." Now, there's a man for you. Phil has a lot of things on his mind—he's going to be operated on tomorrow —but he didn't want Ronnie worrying because he had put Phil in the hospital.

We had a light workout at Skateland for tomorrow's third game against the Bruins. It took us about ninety minutes to make the trip by bus from the Westchester Country Club. The guys were pretty loose. I sat in my customary front seat, read a newspaper for a while, and dozed off.

When we got back to the club at around 4:00 P.M., some of the guys wandered over to the putting green. Bobby Rousseau, Mike Murphy, Slats Sather, and I decided to test the course. It's where they hold the Westchester

Classic every summer. We played the first and second holes, then cut across the fairway and played Nos. 17 and 18.

We made a few bets along the way. I was a buck ahead of Bobby and Mike going to No. 18. Slats didn't bet. He couldn't get the zipper to work on his wallet. As I was addressing the ball for my third shot on the par-five eighteenth, somebody yelled, and I pushed the ball into a trap. I had trouble getting out and wound up losing two dollars. It's only money.

Myrna phoned me at the club and told me about a number of newspaper and radio-TV "experts" who had picked us to lose to Boston. Jim Bouton was one of them. Now here's a washed-up pitcher who probably doesn't see three or four hockey games a year and suddenly he's an expert. He went on Channel 7 and made a few snide remarks about me and how I claimed all the pressure would be on the Bruins. I wonder if he's ready to agree with me now? I doubt it. From all I've heard about Bouton, he likes to disagree with everybody. That makes him controversial. It also makes him look like an ass.

APRIL 7

Bep Guidolin—or was it Harry Sinden?—finally decided that the Bruins couldn't win with Jacques Plante in the net. Old Jake looked pretty sad in the first two games, so tonight Eddie Johnston got a chance to start. E.J., which is what most of his buddies call him, was super, and the Bruins won, 4–2.

"I can't remember ever wanting to win a game so much," E.J. said after the game. He wasn't kidding, either. The Bruins had virtually ignored him after getting Plante from Toronto, so this gave E.J. a chance to prove that he can still play pretty good goal.

It was a damn good game. Stemkowski and Ratelle

scored for us. Ratelle's goal tied the score at 2–2 early in the third period. Then, with about ten minutes left, Greg Sheppard beat Giacomin on a breakaway. Eddie made a fast recovery from that pinched nerve in his neck and was able to start. But I'll bet Sheppard's goal gave Eddie another pain in the neck. Sheppard has been playing great hockey. He's been the best Boston forward on the ice.

I had a fight with Sanderson in the second period. Derek likes to chop at you with his stick; he's an expert slasher. I nailed him near the boards and he turned around and whacked me across the back with his stick. I had to show him I wasn't going to take that crap, so I dropped my gloves and took him on.

Some people wonder if fights like this are staged. I can honestly say I've never involved myself in a fight just to excite the fans or liven up a dull game. When I fight it's because I feel I've been wronged and I want revenge, nothing else.

I have also been asked if hockey players exchange any words while they're fighting. Sather talks—yells is a better word—because he wants to distract the other guy or get him so enraged he can't see straight. But I let my fists do the talking. In this particular fight with Sanderson, neither of us said a word. We just punched.

Our loss to Boston didn't upset the guys too much. We had our chances, but E.J. handled most of them. Okay, so we won't sweep the Bruins in four games. We didn't expect to do that anyway, but we do expect to win the series.

We had a chance to renew acquaintances with our wives after the game and check on the health of the kids, etc. After a few beers, the gals went home and we went back to Westchester.

In taping my thoughts on the fight with Sanderson, I was reminded of a story Giacomin told me about his brother,

Rollie, who was at the second game in Boston. Near the end of the game, Rollie got up to cheer the Rangers, and a fan behind him suggested that Rollie sit down. Rollie told the fan to "buzz off." The fan reached down and pulled Rollie's hairpiece off.

"What happened then?" I asked Eddie.

"What do you think?" Eddie said. "Rollie hammered the guy. Then he picked up his hairpiece, placed it back on his head, and walked out of there like the heavyweight champion of the world."

APRIL 8

I wasn't feeling too good when I got up this morning. It's the same old story: headaches, dizziness, weakness. I felt it coming on last night, but I wanted to play, so I didn't mention it to anybody. I spoke to Emile at noon today and told him I wasn't 100 percent or even close to it.

During the warmup before tonight's fourth game I couldn't even shoot the puck. I went to the dressing room, and Emile saw me and scratched me from the lineup. I lay down on the rubbing table in the trainer's room and slept through the entire game. When I got up and joined the guys they were celebrating a 4–0 victory—Giacomin's first play-off shutout of his NHL career.

I was happy for Eddie's sake. This was his forty-fourth play-off game covering seven years, and I'm sure there is no team he'd rather shut out than Boston. He gets an added incentive whenever he plays the Bruins because he hates them.

Eddie got into a skirmish near the end of the game. He came out to clear a loose puck, and Carol Vadnais came up behind him and crosschecked him. Eddie chased Vadnais up the ice, swinging his big goalie stick. Ronnie Harris then dumped Vadnais on his back. I think Vadnais got the message.

Bobby Rousseau did a helluva job filling in for me on the Ratelle line. He drew an assist on a goal by Gilbert with the game only three minutes old. Bobby then beat Ed Johnston with a great slap shot from the right face-off circle in the second period.

Bobby Orr got caught up ice on Rousseau's goal, tried to catch him, but couldn't. I'm sure Orr is having trouble with his knees. He seems to have trouble pivoting, especially when he has to move to his right.

Orr was on the ice during the final two minutes when our guys put on hockey's version of basketball's freeze. The Bruins didn't touch the puck for almost a minute and a half. Orr didn't like that. He said, "The Rangers kind of rubbed it in then, but we didn't do much to stop them."

APRIL 9

I'm feeling better today, but I skipped practice so I could get a little more rest. Then I left with the team for Boston, where we play the fifth game tomorrow night.

I had an interesting conversation with Ronnie Harris on our plane flight to Boston. He was reminding me that he broke into the NHL ten years ago, and this is only the second time he got into the Stanley Cup play-offs.

"It was when I was with Detroit in 1970," Ronnie said. "We got wiped out in four games by Chicago. We lost every game by the same score, 4–2. All those other years I was with teams that weren't good enough to make the play-offs. I had to go home at the end of the regular season and watch the play-offs on TV. Now I'm with a team that has a chance to go all the way and I'm giving it all I have."

Ronnie Harris is my kind of guy. He's a little shy and soft-spoken, but when he's on the ice he gives you 110 percent all the time. He's hitting people and carrying the puck well and giving us that extra zip we've lacked in the past.

You can say the same about Bert Marshall. He figured to be a swing man on defense when Emile picked him up from the Golden Seals, but he's always ready to play. When Dale Rolfe had to sit out the fourth game against the Bruins with an aching left hand, Bert moved in and played a helluva game. He's great at blocking shots and knows how to use his body.

Sather had been showing the guys a letter he received from a young fan. It was from a boy who wrote, "Thanks for the phony autograph picture you sent me, you jerk. Send me a better picture with your proper signature the next time, you jerk."

Now, how did that kid know Glen Sather is a jerk?

APRIL 10

Where are all the skeptics now? Where have you gone, Jim Bouton? Whatever happened to Harry Sinden?

We beat the Bruins, 6–3, tonight. The defending champs are dead—in five games! All New England is in mourning.

Vickers got our first goal after only thirty-eight seconds of play, and that really hurt the Bruins. "Sarge" added two more later in the game, and that really buried the Bruins. For a rookie to score three goals in a play-off game is really something, but Vickers has never acted like a rookie. He plays like he's been in the league for years.

As the game was winding down, the Boston fans started yelling insults at Sinden, who was in his usual seat just to the left of the Boston bench. One guy yelled, "Do something, Harry, before it's too late." Harry just sat there with his chin on his chest. I looked across the ice when there was about a minute left to play and Harry was gone. He couldn't bear to watch the finish.

Sinden had opened his big mouth to a reporter before the series started and claimed the Rangers couldn't win the big games. I found it hard to control my emotions after the game. A TV announcer asked me how we did it and I said, "Harry Sinden was a big help. Our guys read his prediction in the papers and that's all they needed as an incentive."

There were other factors involved, of course. How did we manage to stop Bobby Orr? He got only one goal in the series. Well, there's no point in keeping it a secret now. During our stay at Fitchburg we studied films of our last two regular-season games against the Bruins and we came up with a plan to reduce Bobby's effectiveness.

Have you ever noticed how Orr likes to take the puck behind his own net and then move out? In the past he used to be a threat to go all the way to the other team's blue line before passing. But his bad knees caused him to change his style. He might still give you one or two moves like that during a game, but most of the time he looks to pass off.

Emile decided that on those occasions when Orr led the attack we would watch which route he takes—it's usually the right side—and then flood that area. Two men would encircle him, make him work harder, and put added pressure on him and his weak knees. The third forward on our attacking line would then act like a free safety in football. His job was to anticipate the pass and move in front of the likely receiver. There was some risk involved here because it left an open man on the other side, but we relied on the defense to back us up.

Orr had trouble spotting that open man anyway because of our two forecheckers. And when he tried to pass to the other side, our free safety was there to intercept or knock the receiver off the puck.

We learned something else during our film sessions at

124

Fitchburg. It dealt with Don Awrey, Orr's defensive partner. We noticed that when the other team was on the attack, Awrey normally would rush up from his position at left defense to force the play, leaving Orr to back him up.

This created an open area to Orr's left. Our centers were told to watch for this when carrying the puck. Their objective was to hit the right wing with a pass behind Awrey or simply throw the puck deep into the corner.

So by going to the movies in Fitchburg we found a way to bottle up the Bruins' offense and another way to exploit one of their weaknesses on defense. It all added up to a sweet opening-round victory.

There must have been six thousand fans at LaGuardia Airport when we arrived back from Boston. They wanted to share in our joy, but some of them got too enthusiastic. A lot of the guys had trouble fighting their way through the mob. We finally reached safety by climbing aboard a bus that took us to another section of the airport. Then we made our way to parking lot No. 5, got into our cars, and drove home.

APRIL 11

Giacomin had a hair-raising experience at the airport last night. He said that when the mob descended on him and his wife, Marg, he jumped into a cab and told the driver to take them to the parking lot. But the driver had trouble maneuvering his cab through the crowd. Some fans jumped on the hood and roof. Others started rocking the cab and pounding on the windows. By this time, Marg was crying, and the driver was fearful that the fans would overturn the cab.

Eddie finally got out of the cab. He was holding a bottle of liquor that a fan had given him when he got off the plane. He told the fans to "cool it" and let the cab move on.

125

"Then one guy called me a guinea or something that sounded like that and I lost my cool," Eddie said. "I threw the bottle into the crowd, got back into the cab, and told the driver to take off. I said, 'The hell with my car . . . take me home and I'll pick it up here tomorrow.' The cab fare was sixteen dollars to Manhasset, but it was worth it to get away from those maniacs."

When Eddie finished his story, I thought about it for a while and said, "I don't think I could face that again. We'd better make sure we win the Cup at home."

We could have used a rest after the Boston series, but we didn't get it. We practiced this morning at Skateland, then caught a plane for Chicago. Our semifinal series against the Black Hawks opens tomorrow night at Chicago Stadium. The other semifinal series will pit the Canadiens against the Flyers.

The Black Hawks needed only five games to eliminate the St. Louis Blues. Tony Esposito is hot as a firecracker. He worked Chicago's four winning games and gave up only four goals—an average of one a game. Whew! That's some goaltending.

On the eve of our series opener against Boston, Sheldon Kannegiesser, the spare defenseman we picked up from Pittsburgh, said grace when we gathered for dinner. Emile, being a superstitious man, suggested Sheldon offer another prayer before dinner tonight. Sheldon again said grace. He's a very religious person and a student of the Bible. He's also a gentleman. He saw only brief service in one play-off game against the Bruins, but you never hear him complain.

APRIL 12

Kannegiesser watched our first game against the Black Hawks from the press box, but he still played a part in our

4–1 victory. Well, one of his sticks did. My sticks didn't feel right during the pregame warmup. I went to the bench and grabbed one of Sheldon's. It felt lighter and more comfortable, so I decided to try it out in the game. I was still using it when I beat Tony Esposito from a tough angle early in the third period. It broke a 1–1 tie and turned out to be the winner. Thanks, Shelly.

Tkaczuk added two goals, one into an empty net, and Rousseau got our other goal with a forty-foot slapper. My goal was a tremendous morale booster. It was my first in six play-off games. Ratelle fed me a lead pass after I got behind Bill White, the Chicago defenseman, and let it go from the outer edge of the left face-off circle. It beat Esposito on the far side.

"I should have stopped it," Tony moaned later. "It was a bad goal."

Maybe it looked bad to you, Tony, but it looked awfully good to me.

Giacomin was brilliant again tonight. The only shot he missed was one by Pit Martin in the first period. That shot whistled off Eddie's glove and landed in the net. Eddie has now led us to five victories in six play-off games in a span of eight nights. Not bad goaltending, heh?

APRIL 13

We switched hotels today. I hope it doesn't change our luck. We had been staying out at the airport at the O'Hare International Tower, a new hotel owned by the Madison Square Garden Corporation. But Emile didn't like all the commuting time we were putting in. For instance, it took us almost ninety minutes to get from the hotel to Chicago Stadium for last night's game and about the same time to travel back to the hotel.

After today's noon practice at the Stadium we checked

into Executive House. It's close to the Loop and to all those good shops on Michigan Avenue. If we had remained at the airport we would have died of boredom waiting for Sunday afternoon's second game.

George Shearing is appearing at London House up the street. Some of the jazz buffs among us plan to catch his early show tonight.

APRIL 14

A nice day for a ball game, so after today's practice Emile piled into a cab with some of the writers and went to old Comiskey Park to watch the White Sox play the Kansas City Royals. The Cat is an old semipro baseball player and manager. He has maintained his interest in the game and can quote all the major league statistics, who're the leading hitters and pitchers, etc.

I chatted with Dennis Hull and Stan Mikita at the Stadium this morning. Denny was in a joking mood. He said, "Hey, Vic, it's nice to see the Cat is letting you practice with the team." Denny hasn't forgotten Moscow and my run-in with Sinden at practice.

Mikita was wearing some jazzy slacks with black-and-white stripes. I told him he looked like a two-legged zebra and then asked him what he was having for dinner, figuring he would take the hint and invite me to his house.

"Spaghetti and meatballs," Stan said. "Want to join us?"

"No thanks," I said. "The Rangers eat only steaks."

Stan chuckled. "You guys are too damn rich," he said.

APRIL 15

Pat Stapleton and I are old friends. We were roomies during our Junior amateur days in the Black Hawks' organization. Then we went our separate ways. The Hawks left me unprotected in the 1961 draft and the Rangers grabbed me; Chicago lost Paddy in the same draft to Boston, then reacquired him four years later.

Paddy and I have remained good friends down through the years, but today I hate him. The little bugger scored two goals and set up one by Dick Redmond in the Hawks' 5–4 victory in the second game.

This was one of those nationally televised Sunday matinee games, and the viewers were treated to plenty of excitement. Paddy's two goals and one by Dennis Hull gave Chicago a 3–0 lead in the first eleven minutes. We bounced back to tie the score before the eighth minute of the second period. It was now Gilles Villemure's game to win or lose. He had relieved Eddie Giacomin at the end of the opening period. Gilly wound up the loser when Hull got his second goal of the afternoon and Stapleton set up Redmond for what turned out to be the decisive goal.

The Hawks lost Keith Magnuson when he threw himself in front of a second-period slap shot by Brad Park. "It caught him square on the jaw," Park said. "Then I heard something crack." It was Magnuson's jawbone.

The force of the shot fractured Magnuson's jaw in two places. The redhead is a tough rascal. After going to a hospital to have the jaw wired, Maggie claimed he'd be back by next weekend, wearing one of those birdcage masks. I doubt it.

APRIL 16

It's good to be back home for a few days. We play the next two games at Madison Square Garden—tomorrow night and Thursday night.

After practice today, some of the guys were sunning themselves outside Skateland. One of them was Villemure, who is very light-skinned. Our nicknames for him include "Whitey," "Snowflake," and "Short Ass."

"Be careful you don't get a sunburn, Whitey," I said.

"Yeah, that sun is hot," he said. "I'd better stay in the shade."

Villemure has been sitting in the shade—down at the end of the bench—for most of the play-offs. But when he gets the call, as he did Sunday when Giacomin was yanked after one period, little Gilly is always ready. I imagine he'd like to get a start in these play-offs, and maybe he will. In the meantime, he works hard in practice to stay in shape and never frets or worries. He has the perfect temperament for a goaltender.

APRIL 17

Another great game, but we didn't win. The Hawks got a flukey goal by Jim Pappin and a good goal by Stan Mikita to beat us, 2–1, in the third game. We had enough opportunities, outshooting Chicago, 38–28, but Tony Esposito kept making the big saves. The only one he missed was a great effort by Tkaczuk in the second period.

Pappin scored at the end of a two-on-one breakaway with Hull in the first period. Pappin wasn't even going for the net. He threw the puck across the goalmouth to Hull, the puck struck Jim Neilson's right skate and landed in the net. What luck.

I've never been a great Pappin admirer. He's a little lackadaisical and backs away from the rough stuff. It bugged me to see him get credit for that goal.

Mikita's goal was something else. He fought like hell for the puck along the left boards, gave it to John Marks, and headed for the net. Marks' shot came in low, and Giacomin stopped it. Mikita, standing to Eddie's right, grabbed the rebound and hoisted in it. Give Stan an "A" for effort on that one.

Billy Reay barred the press from the Chicago dressing room after the game. Well, not really. He told the writers that J. P. Bordeleau, a seldom-used forward, would serve as the "designated speaker" for the club. The other members of the Hawks were ordered not to speak to the press. It was a "bush" trick on Reay's part, and I'm sure many of the Chicago players were embarrassed by their coach's action.

APRIL 18

Stemkowski was needling Villemure at practice today. Villemure has totaled only sixty-one minutes of play-off action thus far. "Hey, Gilly, you're in the running for the Conn Smythe Trophy," Stemkowski said, referring to the play-offs' Most Valuable Player award. Gilly laughed off the remark.

Our series with the Hawks, though, is no laughing matter. We lost the home ice advantage when Chicago beat us last night. We'll really be in trouble if we don't bounce back on our home ice tomorrow night.

I telephoned Andy Bathgate today in Oakville. He and my brother, Carl, have been working hard to get our golf course in shape for the new season. "Keep up the good work and I'll give you guys some of my play-off money," I said.

"Is that a promise?" Andy asked.

"It's a promise," I said.

"Then beat hell out of the Black Hawks," Andy said.

That's what we intend to do, but the Hawks hold a 2–1 edge in games now and figure to get tougher as the series moves along.

APRIL 19

The starting times for our games at the Garden have been set back to 9:00 P.M. in order to permit the circus to stage two shows a day. This has screwed up things for most of us. We're getting to bed later and getting up later and hav-

131

ing our pregame steak later than usual. It's almost like playing on the West Coast.

Our pregame meeting today was scheduled for 12:30 P.M. I drove into the city with the usual gang—Sather, Neilson, MacGregor, and Marshall. We arrived about fifteen minutes late because of an accident in the Midtown Tunnel that backed up the traffic. Emile didn't rip us for being late; he's wound up in those traffic jams himself and knows what it's like.

During our meeting in the dressing room, we looked at films of our Sunday game against the Black Hawks. I got so absorbed in the movie that I didn't pay any attention to Sather, who was sitting next to me. When the lights came on, the back of my shirt was covered with foot powder. I knew who the culprit was. That's an old Sather trick.

Most of the guys were real loose before the game. Stemkowski went through his usual dressing-room ritual of standing on his head for about a minute. He claims it helps stir up the blood. Every time I watch him do that I laugh and say, "Well, Stemmer, you look a lot better standing on your head than on your skates."

Other guys have methods of getting ready for a game that border on superstition. Sather likes to limber up on the stationary bike, then he goes through a series of exercises to stretch his back muscles. He doesn't bother standing on his head, though.

Frank Paice, the trainer, finds out which goaltender is playing. He then gets a puck, puts it between his knees, waddles over to the goalie, and releases the puck so that it drops into the goalie's catching glove. That tips us off on which goaltender is starting, because Emile never announces his lineup ahead of time.

I'm not superstitious, so I just sit on my foot locker near the door, counting the minutes and praying that we will all play well and that nobody will be injured.

Nobody suffered any physical injuries tonight, but we

132

all were hurt inside when the Hawks beat us, 3–1, in the fourth game. One more loss and the season will be over for the Rangers.

Giacomin and Esposito put on another exciting goal-tending duel. Dennis Hull broke a scoreless tie with a power-play goal in the eleventh minute of the second period. I tied the score with a rebound shot early in the third period. Now the Garden crowd of 17,500 was cheering us on because it looked like we had the Hawks on the run.

But with less than six minutes left to play, Pit Martin took off on a breakaway. He waited until he reached the left face-off circle and fired a shot that went between Giacomin's pads. Hull's second goal of the game almost three minutes later clinched it for the Hawks.

What the hell is wrong with us? Giacomin has been playing great goal, but we're giving up too many break-aways. He can't stop all of them. Just before Martin's goal, Eddie made a great sprawling save on a breakaway by Jim Pappin.

Eddie was fit to be tied when it was over. He said, "Damn, we give Pappin that breakaway and I guess that wasn't good enough, so we turn around and give another one to Martin. Damn."

Damn is right. We always seem to give the Hawks that first goal and then we have to play catch-up. We become overaggressive with our forechecking, take chances, get a little sloppy, and that sets up the breakaways.

The fifth game was scheduled for Sunday—Easter Sunday—but has been postponed until Tuesday night. That gives us four days to lick our wounds. We can use it.

APRIL 21

Went to the race track today with Bruce MacGregor and two of our friends, Joe Rugnetta and Pete DeStefano. We laid a few shillings on a horse owned by Joe. His name is Doc Gibson. Doc won and paid $10.80 for $2.00.

Maybe our luck is starting to change.

APRIL 22

This is the first Easter Sunday I've been able to spend with the family in seven years. Sather and Marshall dropped in during the afternoon and we watched the Montreal-Philadelphia game on TV. The Canadiens won to open a 3–1 lead in that semifinal series. Now the Flyers are in the same boat with us. One more defeat and the season is over for them.

APRIL 23

Some of those Chicago writers make me laugh. They turned their backs on the Black Hawks when we won the series opener. Now they're singing a different tune. I picked up a couple of newspapers after we checked into Executive House tonight, and all the writers are predicting that the Hawks will wrap up the series in tomorrow night's fifth game. Front-runners, that's what they are.

We went to the movies after dinner. No, it wasn't a skin flick. We gathered in a meeting room in the hotel and looked at films of our fourth game against Chicago. It hurt to see the number of chances we blew, including one I had in the second period. Esposito was sprawled on the ice when I got the puck to his right. I had almost the whole net to shoot at and I popped it over the net. I got it up so high I couldn't believe it stayed inside the rink.

The guys didn't do much talking while watching the film. We're in trouble now and we know it. How do you wipe out a 3–1 deficit in games? "We're going to have to work our asses off tomorrow night," Park said when we returned to our room.

134

Okay, Porky. We'll work our asses off and then try to find a way to beat Tony Esposito.

It's all over, including the shouting. The Black Hawks beat us, 4–1, last night to earn the right to play Montreal in the Stanley Cup final. We flew home after the game, and it was a lot different from the greeting we got after the Boston series. Nobody showed up at the airport except our wives and a few curious airline mechanics.

How could the Black Hawks wipe us out in five games after we played so well against the Bruins? There were several reasons. First, Tony Esposito was fantastic. He gave up only three goals in the last three games. As the Cat said, "You don't win many games scoring only one goal a game." How true.

Our power play also failed us. We scored only one power-play goal out of thirteen attempts during the series. Chicago had four out of thirteen, including one by Stan Mikita last night that put us in a hole in the opening period and caused us to play catch-up the rest of the way. We never caught up.

We also forgot to hit. I feel if we had been half as physical as we were against Boston, we could have beaten the Hawks. They had some guys who were hurting, but we never roughed them up. We backed off and played right into their hands.

Dennis Hull had a big hand in the Hawks' clinching victory with a goal and three assists. His goal in the second period proved to be the winner. I can't remember ever seeing Denny play so well. Maybe that's because he no longer is playing in the shadow of brother Bobby.

Gilbert scored for us just before the end of the second period. It cut Chicago's lead to 2–1 and gave us a big lift. During the intermission between the second and third periods, the guys were real perky and anxious to get back on the ice.

Hockey players always loosen the laces of their skate boots between periods. We usually don't tie them again until Emile enters the room just before the three-minute warning buzzer. But last night the guys were all laced up and ready to go when the boss came through the door.

Emile said, "Let's keep plugging along now and don't take any unnecessary chances. One more goal and we can pull this thing out."

But Dennis Hull ruined it for us. He set up Mikita's second goal of the game early in the final period, then drew an assist on a goal by Cliff Koroll. Vickers was hanging all over Koroll, but Cliff still managed to push the puck under Giacomin's stick.

I felt like somebody had cut off my legs as I sat in the dressing room after the game. But I stopped feeling sorry for myself when Emile entered the room. He was pale and drawn and completely dragged out. This was the man I bled for. He shook every player's hand and offered little condolences like, "Thanks, you gave it your best shot," or "You never quit on me. . . . Thanks a lot."

There were a lot of misty eyes as the Cat made the rounds. I had to blink away the tears when he grabbed my right hand and squeezed it and said, "Thanks, Vic. I guess it wasn't meant to be."

That's the way my twelfth season with the Rangers ended.

It had been a long journey. Eight months of hockey—beginning in August with Team Canada and ending on a mild spring day in April. There were moments of joy and moments of bitterness and frustration.

We didn't win the Stanley Cup and maybe, as Emile Francis said, it wasn't meant to be. But I feel we fought the good fight—and that's what life is all about.